Acting Out Loud

Christian Skits for All Occasions

S. E. Thomas

Yesenia A. Thomas
Illustrator

Acting Out Loud
Christian Skits for All Occasions

Published by The Dramatic Pen Press, L.L.C.

Lolo, Montana

ISBN: 0692329587
ISBN-13: 978-0692329580

For my nephew, Josiah Paul Thomas.
May you continue to share the love of Jesus Christ
with the people around you in your typical eager,
thoughtful, and compassionate way.

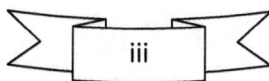

CONTENTS

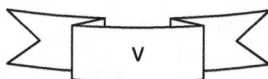

ACKNOWLEDGEMENTS

I would like to thank Pastor Dan Bailey and the congregation of Trinity Baptist Church of Moscow, Idaho. Pastor Dan allowed me to use the congregation there as guinea pigs for my various dramatic pursuits, and they responded with great forbearance and encouragement. It is my sincerest wish that these materials bless other congregations and drama teams as they creatively try to spread the message of Christ's deep love.

⤮ SECTION ONE ⤮

Biblical Skits

Elijah and the Widow
A Modern Retelling

Theme:
God's Provision

Setting:
A humble living room.

Props/Decorations:
A pitcher
A mixing bowl
Mixing spoon or whisk
Three chairs set up to loosely resemble a living room
Two bread rolls.
A small table or tray table. Put the pitcher, mixing bowl, and mixing spoon on the table. Hide bread rolls in the bowl.

Key Verses:
I Kings 17

Time Duration:
5-7 minutes

Characters:
ELIJAH   Dressed like a bum.
WIDOW
SON

Script:

[ENTER WIDOW and SON. They are sitting in the living room together.]

SON

[Holding stomach.]
Mom, I'm so hungry! We haven't eaten for days! When are we going to eat?

WIDOW

I'm sorry son. I keep hoping and praying for God to provide for us, but my prayers go unanswered. I'm beginning to wonder if He hears me at all.

[ENTER ELIJAH]

SOUND: KNOCKING ON DOOR

WIDOW

Who could that could be?

SON

Maybe it's God, answering your prayers.

WIDOW

Or, it could be someone selling vacuum cleaners.
[Stands and answers door.]
Hello. Who are you?

ELIJAH

I am Elijah, a prophet of the Most High God.

WIDOW

[Skeptical.]
Oh, is that so?

ELIJAH

Yes. He told me to come to this home. Would you please bring me some water?

[WIDOW turns to get the water.]

ELIJAH

And, could you bring me something to eat, too?

12

WIDOW

Look, Mr. Prophet, whatever your name is. I am happy to bring you some water, but I have nothing left to eat. No bread—only a little flour and the smallest bit of oil. Once that is gone, my son and I will starve!

ELIJAH

Do not be afraid to do as I say. Please, make me a small cake from your oil and flour and then make another for your son and for yourself. The Most High God has promised He will provide for us. For as long as this famine continues, your flour and oil will not be used up.

WIDOW

But how can that be?

ELIJAH

Nothing is impossible with God.

WIDOW

[Seems to be considering for a moment.]
Very well. I will do as you say. After all, I have only God on whom to rely. Please, come in.

[ELIJAH enters and sits down with the boy. WIDOW pretends to make some rolls. WIDOW gives one roll to ELIJAH. WIDOW sits with them and she and SON share the other roll. They all eat hungrily.]

SON

Mom, that was really good! But I'm still really hungry!

WIDOW

I'm sorry, but I'm certain I used the rest of the flour and oil. There is none left.

ELIJAH

Recall what I told you. The Most High God will not let your oil and flour run out. Go check again.

[WIDOW gets up and goes back. She looks into the jug and bowl and is amazed to find more flour and oil there.]

WIDOW

[Amazed.]
You are right! There is more of both!

SON

Can you make me some more rolls, then, Mom?

WIDOW

Yes! I can!

ELIJAH

Don't forget about me! I want one, too! …Um, make that four!
[Smiles and pretends to start cooking again.]

[EXIT ELIJAH, WIDOW, and SON.]

THE END

Fashioned by God

Setting:
This is designed to be a fashion show. Women dress in character and walk down a runway as the narrator reads about them and as the appropriate hymn plays in the background. After taking their walk, they line up together at one end of the stage until the end.

Music:
"Have I Done My Best for Jesus?" "Wherever He Leads, I'll Go." "My Faith Has Found a Resting Place." "I Am Bound For the Promised Land." "Stayed Upon Jehovah." *Optional Special Music:* "God Has a Plan for Everyone."

Time Duration:
20-25 minutes

Characters:

NARRATOR: Will read the entire script. No other characters have any lines.

LYDIA: Dressed in purple & red biblical garb. Perhaps carrying a small vial of something purple. (Acts 16:11-15, 40)

NAOMI: An older woman dressed in plain, biblical garb, carrying a clay jug. (The Book of Ruth.)

RUTH: A young woman dressed in plain, biblical garb and carrying a basket of wheat. (The Book of Ruth & Matthew 1:5)

RAHAB: A young woman dressed in fancy, biblical garb. Lots of jewelry and bright colors. (Joshua 2:9a & 11b)

JOCHEBED: | A middle-aged woman dressed in tattered biblical garb, carrying a large basket. (Exodus 2, 6:20, Numbers 26:59)

MIRIAM: | A young woman/teen wearing tattered biblical garb, carrying long reed or cattail. (Exodus 2 & 15, Numbers 12)

QUEEN ESTHER: | A woman dressed in royal, biblical garb. She wears a crown and jewelry and carries a scepter. (The Book of Ester)

Script:

NARRATOR

"The Lord God said, 'It is not good for man to be alone. I will make a helper suitable for him.' ...So the Lord God caused the man to fall into a deep sleep; and while he was sleeping, he took one of the man's ribs and closed up the place with flesh. Then the Lord God made a woman from the rib he had taken out of the man, and he brought her to him. The man said, 'This is now bone of my bones and flesh of my flesh; she shall be called woman, for she was taken out of man.'" Genesis 2:18, 21-23

How beautiful Eve must have appeared to Adam when, after all of his searching, he was finally rewarded with a being *fashioned by God* especially for him! What was it that drew him to her? Her outward appearance or her heart? The Bible has many examples for us of women of great character. So, today we'd like to meet a few of them in a fashion show of sorts—a show that, while letting us glimpse a bit of what their outward *fashions* might have been, will also give us a deeper look at how God so intricately *fashioned* their character.

[BEGIN MUSIC: "Have I Done My Best for Jesus?"]

Scripture tells us that Paul's conquest of Europe started at a riverside with one convert—a woman named Lydia.

[ENTER LYDIA STAGE RIGHT. She slowly begins her trip down the catwalk, fashion-show style, as the narrator reads. At the end of the reading, she should be standing at STAGE LEFT, quietly waiting for the others.]

In a day when men ruled with strict sovereignty and women had few rights—even over their own children, Lydia successfully took her place alongside men in business. Her shrewdness and personal charm drew people to her; her sincerity and integrity made them trust her.

The first thing Scripture tells us about Lydia is that she was "seller of purple". She was most likely a widow who had courageously and capably carried on her husband's trade for the sake of her children. She knew her product well. She was skilled in procuring the precious dyes and in bringing out the brilliant hues in the textiles she created. There were no colors as gorgeous as the crimsons and purples of Thyatira, her hometown. And Lydia, an enterprising businesswoman, knew the secrets of the Tyrian tint that made the vibrant reds and the rich purples the royalty loved so much.

It is very likely that Lydia advertised her products by wearing them herself. How beautiful she must have looked as she walked through the market square with royal grace and dignity! In Acts 16:14, we learn that the Lord opened her heart and she believed when Paul spoke of Christ's crucifixion—of how His crimson blood washed away all iniquity. How poignant this message must have been to Lydia who, every time she glanced one of her beautiful garments, was reminded of Christ's redeeming love for her! How could she keep silent? She could not! She took the message back home and shared Christ's love with her children and her servants. Soon, her whole household was saved! And then, longing to be of service to Christ's messengers, she pleaded with Paul. "If you have judged me to be faithful," she said, "come to my house and make it your home."

[MUSIC FADE OUT. LYDIA is now at STAGE LEFT, waiting quietly for the others to join her. BEGIN MUSIC: "Wherever He Leads, I'll Go."]

The book of Ruth is one of the briefest in the Bible, but in this love story we behold the attractiveness of virtue, the beauty of sacrifice, and the power of simple trust in God.

[ENTER NAOMI STAGE RIGHT. She slowly begins her trip down the catwalk, fashion-show style, as the narrator reads. At the end of the reading, she should be standing at STAGE LEFT, quietly waiting for the others.]

Naomi and her husband, Elimelech, moved from Bethlehem to Moab with their two sons. It was not easy living among a pagan people, but when Elimelech died, leaving Naomi to raise their two sons alone, life became unbearable. Money was tight, support was hard to find, and spiritual counsel was nonexistent. Still, Naomi persevered for the sake of her children. As Naomi struggled through her sorrow and fear, God showed her, day by day, that He was her refuge, her strength, and her comfort.

Naomi's sons grew to age and, since they were living in Moab, chose Moabite wives. Naomi must have been saddened and full of regret by her sons' marriages to heathen girls, but in her grace and good sense, she took these young ladies into her heart and home. Then, tragedy struck again when both of Naomi's sons were also taken from her. Now she was a childless widow in a strange land. Naomi remembered, though, how God had been faithful to her when Elimelech had passed, so she grasped onto His hand of comfort and strength once again. Through faith, Naomi again took on the responsibility for her small family—that now consisted of herself and her two Moabite daughters-in-law.

[NAOMI is now at STAGE LEFT, waiting quietly for the others to join her. ENTER RUTH STAGE RIGHT. She slowly begins her trip down the catwalk, fashion-show style, as the narrator reads. At the end of the reading, she should be standing at STAGE LEFT, quietly waiting for the others.]

The Bible does not describe Ruth's appearance, but art and literature have made her extremely lovely. One author pictures her as being "startlingly beautiful"—with dark red hair, high cheek bones, warm eyes, and dressed in the clinging robes of a temple priestess. But it is the appeal of her lovely character that causes us to create such a beautiful picture of Ruth. And though the world would not consider Ruth to be spectacular or heroic, it is the beauty of her heart, her uncomplaining meekness, and her self-sacrificing spirit of loyalty which draws us to her.

Naomi longed for her people and the home of her youth in Bethlehem. She urged her two daughters-in-law, Ruth and Orpah, to seek happiness anew where they could best find it—in their own land and with their own families. Orpah returned to her father's house to forever remain in the heathen land, but Ruth had been deeply touched by Naomi's godly strength, wisdom, and love. Ruth knew she needed Naomi—she needed what Naomi had—a personal, life-giving relationship with the Creator. So she begged, "Don't urge me to leave you or to turn back from you. Where you go I will go, and where you stay I will stay. Your people will be my people and your God my God. Where you die I will die, and there I will be buried. May the Lord deal with me ever so severely, if anything but death separates you and me." (Ruth 1:16-17)

Ruth gave up what could have been a much easier life in Moab in order to break her back gleaning in the fields near Bethlehem for enough food to support both herself and Naomi. Eventually, she found herself working in the field of a man named Boaz, and often mentioned him to Naomi in their quiet evenings together. Naomi, who spent many hours alone in thought as she tidied up their small shack, washed and mended clothing, and made the bread for their meals, knew that Boaz was pleased with Ruth and that Ruth was attracted to Boaz. But Naomi also knew another vital piece of information; Boaz was a distant relative of her husband's... and there was a strange old custom that had the potential to turn the tide of sorrow and loss into a wellspring of joy and prosperity.

Through Naomi's prayers, wisdom, and good advice, Ruth eventually became Boaz's wife. Boaz redeemed Ruth into the family of God's people, and her desire to be one of them in faith and fellowship was finally realized. Many generations later, God rewarded her in the most wonderful way possible, when she became the grandmother of Jesse, the great-grandmother of King David, and a prominent ancestor of Jesus Himself—the Savior of all mankind.

[RUTH is now at STAGE LEFT, waiting quietly for the others to join her. FADE OUT MUSIC. BEGIN MUSIC: "My Faith Has Found a Resting Place."]

The Canaanites were an idolatrous people whose worship was sensuous and atrociously cruel. Their cup of iniquity was full. It was among these people that Rahab lived—in Jericho, the strongest of fortified cities.

> [ENTER RAHAB STAGE RIGHT. She slowly begins her trip down the catwalk, fashion-show style, as the narrator reads. At the end of the reading, she should be standing at STAGE LEFT, quietly waiting for the others.]

Though Rahab had spent her life as a harlot, God sent godly men—His spies—to her home seeking her protection. Rahab's house occupied a place on the city wall and, because the city authorities often saw strange men entering her home, the spies found a measure of safety there. When the king's guards finally began to suspect that all was not as it seemed, Rahab risked her life to hide the spies under some flax on her roof. Then, using a scarlet cord as a signal, Rahab not only aided the Israelites, but saved her family and household from destruction. How? By her faith. She told the spies, "I know that the Lord has given this land to you… the Lord your God is God in heaven above and on the earth below."

As promised, Rahab and her family were rescued before the destruction of Jericho. God's people took her into their fellowship, and she became one of them. She married Salmon and became the mother of Boaz—husband to Ruth. Thus, Rahab, the former harlot, became one of our Lord's ancestors—showing the world that salvation is not dependent on human goodness, but on His free grace to sinners. This example of how God redeemed and elevated a sinful woman shows us how we should never look down with disdain upon others because of their sins. We must forgive, encourage, and love—remembering with humility that God has also forgiven us. God had been working in Rahab's heart, and she truly believed in Him. James says that her faith was living, for it was proven through her actions. She chose God's side and dared to stand alone—for she knew she was secure with the Almighty.

> [RAHAB is now at STAGE LEFT, waiting quietly for the others to join her. FADE OUT MUSIC. BEGIN MUSIC: "I Am Bound For the Promised Land."]

We have all heard the story of how Moses' mother placed him in a basket of reeds to save him from death at the hands of Pharaoh's men. However, we have been told little about the woman who saved him—his mother, Jochebed.

[ENTER JOCHEBED STAGE RIGHT. She slowly begins her trip down the catwalk, fashion-show style, as the narrator reads. At the end of the reading, she should be standing at STAGE LEFT, quietly waiting the others to join her.]

When Pharaoh realized how quickly his Israelite slaves were increasing in number, he became very afraid. If they were to revolt, it could mean civil war, panic, destruction—not to mention an everlasting blight on his reign. So he issued a decree, "Every boy that is born you must throw into the Nile, but let every girl live."

How frightened Jochebed and her family must have been when Moses was born—a healthy baby boy. For three months she was able to hide him—but she knew it was only a matter of time before he was found and ripped from her arms. She had seen it happen to her friends and neighbors, and her sleep was filled with terrors of what might very soon become their plight. So, she began formulating a plan.

Jochebed and her daughter, Miriam, painstakingly prepared the pitch-covered basket of papyrus plants. Finally, when it was ready, they wrapped up little Moses and placed him inside. How she must have wept and prayed as they sent the little one adrift on the great Nile! It seems like a desperate and risky attempt to save the young child. Yet Jochebed trusted in God and in His great provision. Her creativity, resourcefulness, and willingness to risk her life for the life of her child makes her worthy of our honor and respect. But above all, we honor Jochebed for her faith in the love, power, and providence of the true God.

[JOCHEBED is now at STAGE LEFT, waiting quietly for the others to join her. ENTER MIRIAM. She slowly begins her trip down the catwalk, fashion-show style, as the narrator reads. At the end of the reading, she should be standing at STAGE LEFT, quietly waiting for the others.]

Miriam grew up in bondage, under incredible hardship. Despite all of this, her spirit was not broken. When her mother, Jochebed, placed Miriam's baby brother, Moses, in the reed basket on the river, Miriam watched it closely from the riverbank, following it down stream, to be sure no evil befell him. How frightened she must have been when the child was discovered by the daughter of the very man who was trying to rid Goshen of Israelite babies! How she must have prayed for his deliverance! God heard her and answered her prayers—not only delivering Moses, but delivering all of Miriam's people through him.

Miriam grew up to become a brilliant woman and a prophetess of God. She was also extremely interested in the building of a new nation. It appears Miriam never married, but rather dedicated her life to the building of God's kingdom through His chosen people. In their hour of triumph, Moses led 600,000 men in joyous song of victory, and Miriam led an equal number of women. What a glorious view it must have been to see her at the head of Israel's women— leading a beautiful chorus of praise to God.

Later, Miriam made the mistake of allowing envy to creep into her soul. In her weakness, she spoke against her brother, Moses. Her desire for even greater political power brings to light the limitations of her character. God looked into her heart and rebuked her. He put his mark of displeasure on her, and in a moment she was covered with horrible leprosy. She who coveted honor was now in dishonor. It was in answer to Moses's prayer—the one she had wronged—that Miriam was restored to health and to fellowship with her people. Even though Miriam did not see the Promised Land, she will sing again in heaven with the host of the redeemed.

[MIRIAM is now at STAGE LEFT, waiting quietly for the others to join her. ENTER QUEEN ESTHER. She slowly begins her trip down the catwalk, fashion-show style, as the narrator reads. At the end of the reading, she should be standing at STAGE LEFT, quietly waiting for QUEEN ESTHER. MUSIC FADE OUT. BEGIN MUSIC: "Stayed Upon Jehovah."]

Taken into the heart and home of her cousin Mordecai, a Jew of the Tribe of Benjamin, Hadassah grew up to be superbly beautiful.

[ENTER QUEEN ESTHER. She slowly begins her trip down the catwalk, fashion-show style, as the narrator reads. At the end of the reading, she should be standing at STAGE LEFT.]

King Ahasuerus's combed every province of his empire for its most beautiful women. One of the king's men saw Hadassah and, because of her astounding beauty, he selected her to accompany the other young ladies to the palace to participate in a beauty pageant of sorts. However, the winner of this contest would win more than a tin crown and a bundle of roses. She would wed King Ahasuerus and inherit the title of Queen of Persia.

The king's eyes roamed the line of dazzling beauties—but only one of them stood out. Was it the rich robes she wore and her physical charm that attracted him? Or, perhaps it was something far more rare. Only King Ahasuerus knows what made Hadassah shine above all others. His choice fell on her, and she relinquished her Hebrew name to be given a Persian one—Esther, meaning "star". And a star Esther was—shining not only in physical beauty, but in the character of her heart.

Esther and Mordecai wondered why God had allowed her—a Jewish woman, devoted to her family and to God—to be taken by a heathen king. But soon God's plan became piercingly clear. Ahasuerus, not knowing of Esther's true heritage, was tricked by Haman into ordering the merciless slaughter of all the Jewish people in Persia. Esther was greatly troubled. She knew that, even as the queen, her powers were very limited. In great distress, she poured out her fears to the cousin who had raised her. Mordecai, in his wisdom, answered her, "…who knows but that you have come to royal position for such a time as this?" (Esther 4:14b) Esther knew she must go to the king to try to save her people, even though to do so would put her life in jeopardy. She reported back to Mordecai, "Go, gather together all the Jews who are in Susa, and fast for me. Do not eat or drink for three days, night or day. I and my maids will fast as you do. When this is done, I will go to the king, even though it is against the law. And if I perish, I perish." (Esther 4:16)

Despite the cold lump of fear residing in her chest, Esther made herself as attractive as possible, and then walked in all her beauty into the king's court. Upon seeing his dazzling queen kneeling in humility before him, King Ahasuerus did not react with anger at her risky breech of protocol. Indeed, he was impressed to see such courage and sincerity residing beneath her lovely outward appearance.

God's plan for Esther's life was realized in that moment. For not only had God given her an outer beauty to rival all others and win the heart of a king, He had also given her the inner beauty of faith and courage. King Ahasuerus listened to her requests, and then he changed the law, punished the enemies of the Jews, and spared the Jewish race from annihilation—all because of one young lady who was willing to give her life to serve the Lord.

[QUEEN ESTHER is now at STAGE LEFT, waiting with the others.]

Let us conclude our "Fashioned By God" fashion show with a final thought. Through the Bible we learn that God chose these and many other women to fulfill His purposes. From those of the humblest of circumstances to the highest levels of society, from those of sinful backgrounds to the most steadfastly faithful, from those of pagan lands to those of His own chosen people, God had a plan for them all. And when they turned their eyes upon the Lord, His plan for them was realized. He clothed their hearts in faith and they followed Him—regardless of the price. Through their courage and obedience, not only were their lives and families touched by God's grace, but the courses of nations were swayed. Let us always remember that to be within God's plan is a great honor, indeed, and may we trust in God and be found faithful in the plan He has for us.

[EXIT ALL. MUSIC FADE OUT.]

THE END

I CAN'T BEAR THIS!

Setting:

This play contains two settings, one modern and one Biblical. The modern scene will be played out near the pulpit between the Pastor and a congregation member. The Biblical scene will be set further back on stage. It is the scene of Paul during one of his many prison stays and after a severe flogging.

Key Verses:

I Corinthians 1:7-11 "And our hope for you is firm, because we know that just as you share in our sufferings, so also you share in our comfort. We do not want you to be uninformed, brothers, about the hardships we suffered in the province of Asia. We were under great pressure, far beyond our ability to endure, so that we despaired even of life. Indeed, in our hearts we felt the sentence of death. But this happened that we might not rely on ourselves but on God, who raises the dead. He has delivered us from such a deadly peril, and he will deliver us. On him we have set our hope that he will continue to deliver us, as you help us by your prayers. Then many will give thanks on our behalf for the gracious favor granted us in answer to the prayers of many." (See also: Acts 16 & II Corinthians 11:16-33)

Time Duration:

5-7 minutes

Characters:

PASTOR: The pastor of a small church.

SALLY/ETHAN: A congregation member. (Gender doesn't matter.)

PAUL: The Biblical apostle. Dressed in dirty rags and covered in wounds. Looks like he was just beaten severely.

PRISONER: A fellow prisoner with Paul. He, too, is dressed in rags, but has not been beaten recently.

Script:

[ENTER PAUL and PRISONER. They are in the background. PRISONER is sitting on the ground. PAUL is lying on the ground not moving. ENTER PASTOR. PASTOR is standing near the pulpit, gathering his notes and getting ready to leave. ENTER SALLY/ETHAN, who approaches PASTOR.]

SALLY/ETHAN
Pastor, hi. I'm glad I caught you. I have a problem I'd like to discuss with you.

PASTOR
I'm sorry to hear that, SALLY/ETHAN. I'm happy to help if I can.

SALLY/ETHAN
Well, it's just that, in your sermon today, you read a verse and I think you must've read it wrong.

PASTOR
Hm! That *is* serious. But you could be right. Which verse was it?

SALLY/ETHAN
It was I Corinthians 10:13. You read it to say that we won't be *tempted* beyond what we can bear, but I've always heard it quoted as if we won't be asked to *suffer* more than we can bear. I really prefer the latter, because that means that God will protect us Christians from the really bad stuff.

PASTOR
Well, I think we'd better see what the Bible actually says.
[Thumbs through the Bible and finds the verse. He holds it so that SALLY/ETHAN can see for themselves what it says.]
Here we are. It says, "No *temptation* has seized you except what is common to man. And God is faithful; he will not let you be *tempted*

26

beyond what you can bear. But when you are *tempted*, he will also provide a way out so that you can stand up under it."

SALLY/ETHAN
I'm sorry, Pastor, but even though I can see the verse for myself, and I know you were right, I really don't like it! I mean, I always thought that, if we truly believed in Jesus, He'd do a little extra for us—you know, keep us from suffering as much as other people.

PASTOR
Well, think about what the early believers went through. Think about Paul.

LIGHTING: Switch scenes so that the focus in now on the prison scene.

PRISONER
Hey, are you okay? Hey, buddy... can you hear me?
[Sigh. To himself:]
Great! They've killed another one and left the body to rot in my cell!

[PAUL groans and moves just a bit.]

PRISONER
Hey, you're alive! Wake up. You okay?

[PAUL rouses a bit. He tries to push himself up but is in too much pain and remains lying on the ground.]

Easy, there! Take it slow. I've endured their floggings before, too. I thought I would die. But I've never gotten beaten as badly as you have today. You must have done something pretty bad to get them *that* angry! ...Say... what was your crime, anyway?

PAUL
[Speaking with great difficulty. In obvious pain.]
I dared... preach that Jesus Christ is... the Son of God... and our awaited Messiah.

PRISONER

[Whistles and shakes his head.]
Yep. That would do it. I killed my brother. I thought that was bad, but you... you are trying to kill their faith in their gods and in themselves. Very dangerous.

PAUL

This is the fourth... time I have been... given 40 lashes... minus one.

PRISONER

[Shaking head in disbelief.]
I don't know how you're still alive. Or why you keep preaching! Aren't you tired of suffering so much? And, if your God is all that great, why doesn't He protect you?

PAUL

He has protected me. Many times. Too many to count. But God's strength is made perfect in weakness. Often, it is through my weakness... and my suffering... that His strength and glory is seen by the world.

PRISONER

Well, He must have done something pretty amazing for you... or you wouldn't be willing to give up your life for Him again and again.

PAUL

Indeed He did. He gave up His life for me first. ...Someday, my life will end—possibly even this very night—but as long as I have air in my lungs and blood in my veins, I will speak of the sufferings of Jesus Christ.

[Switch scenes back to PASTOR and SALLY/ETHAN.]

PASTOR

See what I mean? Paul was not just a Christian, he was an apostle and one of the very first missionaries. Through Paul, the Gospel of Jesus Christ was spread throughout the Roman Empire. But God did not spare Paul from some very intense suffering. In fact, Paul says in II Corinthians 11:8,

[Reading]
"We do not want you to be uninformed, brothers, about the hardships we suffered in the province of Asia. We were under great pressure, *far beyond our ability to endure*, so that we despaired even of life."

SALLY/ETHAN

Well, I guess, now that I think of it, a good friend of mine once lost a child to cancer. And she is very committed to Jesus. And my brother-in-law—also a Christian—was recently paralyzed in a car accident. So, I guess God doesn't spare Christians from the really bad stuff. In fact, if He did, people might want to come to Jesus for the wrong reasons—to get out of suffering instead of because they actually want a relationship with Him.

PASTOR

Hm… you could be right.

SALLY/ETHAN

And I can see another problem with misreading that verse.

PASTOR

What's that?

SALLY/ETHAN

Well, we can start to think that, if someone is genuinely suffering, that means they're not really a Christian. It could become a reason for us to judge each other instead of help each other.

PASTOR

Right! That would be bad.

SALLY/ETHAN

Thanks, Pastor! I still wish we could be sure we'd never have to suffer much, but it's good to know that, no matter what comes, Jesus is already there. He has walked that road already, and He has proven to me that He loves me enough to be willing to face whatever comes.

PASTOR

And don't forget that He does promise that, if you keep your eyes on Him even when things get tough, He will give you wisdom and spiritual maturity through your sufferings. And one day He will wipe away every tear, for there is no pain on earth that Heaven cannot cure.

[EXIT ALL.]

THE END

Jesus and the Catch of Fish

Setting:
In a boat on the Mediterranean sea, not far from shore.

Key Verses:
John 21:1-14

Props:
A cardboard boat. (Half a boat, actually. Just have people stand behind it to appear they are standing in it.) Two large fishing nets. One is empty and is in the boat. The other is full of large paper fish stuck to it and is hidden behind the boat. (You can use cloth netting for the net.) Consider putting down a blue cloth sheet on part of the stage to represent water under the boat. A small pretend fire (sticks put together to look like a camp fire around flames of red and orange construction paper.)

Time Duration:
5-7 minutes

Characters:

PETER: A fisherman and a disciple of Christ. Dressed in Biblical garb with hem tucked up into belt to make it look like shorts of a sort.

THOMAS: A fisherman and a disciple of Christ. Dressed like Peter.

NATHANEAL: A fisherman and a disciple of Christ. Dressed like Peter.

JOHN: A fisherman and a disciple of Christ. Dressed in a tunic with a belt, untucked.

JESUS: Dressed in traditional Biblical garb.

Script:

[ENTER PETER, THOMAS, NATHANEAL, and JOHN. They are standing in the boat. Peter is holding the empty net. They all look exhausted and dejected.]

PETER
Not one fish! I can't believe it! We've been at it all day and all night. Not one!
[Drops the net in disgust.]

THOMAS
How are we going to feed our families?

NATHANEAL
I have creditors to pay. I can't put them off forever.

[ENTER JESUS on the shore.]

JESUS
[Calling out to them.]
Friends, have you caught any fish?

PETER
[Calling back.]
No. We have fished all night and now it is morning. But we have caught nothing.

JESUS
[Calling out to them.]
Throw your net to the other side of the boat and you will find some.

NATHANEAL
What? How is that supposed to work? Does this man not know fish can swim back and forth beneath the boat?

THOMAS
Who is that man? Why would he say such a thing?

PETER

You are right. It is likely foolishness. But what harm could it do to try? I am so desperate for fish right now I would try anything.

JOHN

Agreed. Let's do it.

[The disciples throw the empty net over the other side (hidden side) of the boat.]

THOMAS

Come, let us pull it back and get back to shore. We tried.

[They strain to pull up the net.]

PETER

What is this? Is it caught on something?

NATHANEAL

I don't believe it! Look, men! Fish!

JOHN

Look at all the fish! There are thousands of them!

PETER

Together, men! Heave!

[After much straining, they manage to pull half of the net full of fish into the boat and then secure it there to tow the rest.]

JOHN
[Looking to shore, he recognizes the man and points.]
It is the Lord!

PETER
[Jumps into the water and runs toward Jesus.]
Jesus! Jesus!
[He embraces Jesus.]

[Other disciples take longer but drag the boat to the shore, along with the fish.]

JESUS
Come, bring some of the fish you have just caught.
[He indicates the campfire.]
We will have breakfast together.

PETER
Again you come to us, my Lord, even though you were dead!

JOHN
Even though I saw your dead body taken and laid in the grave, and we all saw your tomb with the massive stone!

THOMAS
But even I, Thomas, now know to never doubt You again. For You appeared to us in the inner room, and You are indeed here before us today, having conquered death!

[EXIT ALL.]

THE END

JESUS CALMS THE STORM

Theme:
Faith. The lesson Jesus gave about faith being like a mustard seed came immediately before His disciples were tested by the storm at sea.

Setting:
The shoreline of the Sea of Galilee where Jesus just gave a long sermon. The audience is the crowd on the shore and the back part of the stage is the sea.

Props/Decorations:
- Place a large blue sheet or two on the floor of the stage to represent water, leaving a couple of feet of room at the very front of the stage to serve as the shoreline where Jesus stands with His disciples as He preaches.

- Make a large boat out of cardboard—just one side of the boat is enough, so that, when Jesus and the disciples step inside it, there is room for them all, even when Jesus reclines. Position the boat close to the shoreline/edge of blue sheet at first.

- One set of oars

- A mast/sail of some sort would add to the scene greatly and help the actors enact the scene effectively.

- A sound track for lightning crashes will be needed, and consider how you can use the stage lighting to simulate lightning flashes.

Key Verses:
Mark 4:30-41

Time Duration:
5-7 minutes

Characters:

JESUS   Dressed in Biblical garb.
PETER   Dressed in Biblical garb.
ANDREW   Dressed in Biblical garb.
JOHN   Dressed in Biblical garb.

Script:

[ENTER JESUS, ANDREW, PETER, and JOHN. JESUS speaks to the audience as if they are the crowd of people on a hillside, gathering to hear His words.]

JESUS
[He is finishing up his sermon to the people on shore (the congregation).]
And so, I will leave you with this final thought. What shall we say the kingdom of God is like, or what parable shall we use to describe it? It is like a mustard seed, which is the smallest seed you plant in the ground. Yet when planted, it grows and becomes the largest of all garden plants, with such big branches that the birds of the air can perch in its shade. …Now, it is getting late and you must return to your homes and get your children some food.

[JESUS turns to DISCIPLES and indicates the boat and the water.]
Come, my friends, let us go over to the other side.

PETER
Of course, Jesus!
[Motions to Andrew and John.]
Come Andrew. Come John.

[All four men get into the boat. ANDREW rows and PETER and JOHN lift the boat and move it further back, to make it look like they are rowing out to sea. Once there, all four men kneel down in the boat. ANDREW continues to row for a while. Then he tires and PETER takes over.]

JESUS

My friends, it is late and I am very tired. I am going to recline on this cushion and rest for a while.

JOHN

Certainly, my Lord! We will wake you when we reach the other side of the sea.

[JESUS settles down at the back of the boat and goes to sleep. PETER continues to row for a while, then he tires and gives the task to JOHN.]

LIGHTS: FLICKER ON AND OFF

PETER

Did you see that? Lightning!

JOHN

[Pointing.]
And those clouds are piling up in the distance. Look how thick and dark they are! I fear a storm is coming.

SOUND: LIGHTNING CRASH

ANDREW

We must hurry! Row faster, John!

[JOHN rows faster.]

SOUNDS AND LIGHTS: More flickering lights and lightning crashes. Simulate a great storm.

PETER

[Holds up hands, palms up.]
Rain!

[PETER and ANDREW try to cover their heads for a while to simulate trying to stay dry, but eventually give up. The boat starts to rock (actors are rocking it, but not too obviously)   and everyone is swaying back and forth. PETER, ANDREW, and JOHN look terrified.]

ANDREW
The sail! It's tearing!

[PETER tries to fix the sail or bind it to the mast, but can't.]

PETER
It's no use! We've lost it!

JOHN
We're taking on water! I fear the boat will soon sink!

ANDREW
We will all be drowned! We must wake the Teacher!

PETER
I don't know…. I….

SOUNDS AND LIGHTS: More flickering lights and a big lightning crash.

PETER
OK! I will wake Him!
    [Shakes JESUS awake.]
Master, master! Please wake up! How can you sleep? Don't you care if we drown?

SOUNDS AND LIGHTS: More flickering lights and lightning crashes.

JESUS
    [Stands up and puts his arms out. He speaks to the wind and the rain.]
Quiet! Be still!

[No more lightning or flickering lights. The disciples stop rocking the boat and look around in amazement.]

ANDREW

[Amazed.]
The storm! It has passed so suddenly!

[PETER, JOHN, and ANDREW look at JESUS in amazement.]

JESUS

[To all three disciples.]
Why are so you so afraid? Do you still have no faith?
[Disgusted with them, he goes back to his seat and sits down again.]

PETER

[To ANDREW and JOHN.]
Who is this? Even the wind and the waves obey him!

[PETER, JOHN, and ANDREW look at JESUS with fear and amazement. EXIT ALL.]

THE END

OPEN MY EYES

Setting/Theme:
Biblical Dramatic Reading. Decorations optional. Themes: Mercy; Spiritual sight, God's protection.

Key Verses:
II Kings 6:8-23

Time Duration:
5-7 minutes

Characters:

ELISHA'S SERVANT: A man dressed in common Biblical garb.

Script:

[ENTER SERVANT. Snickers, remembering. Reciting or reading from a script.]

SERVANT

The other men and I used to laugh about it over the campfire—how the King of Aram, who like to camp nearby so he could send raiding parties to attack us, used to set up camp in one region or another, but the King of Israel always seemed to know where they were and easily avoided them. We heard stories of how the King of Aram traveled through the ranks of his men, accusing them of being spies and trying to root out the troublemaker. But finally, one man discovered the truth and told the king.

"There is a prophet in Israel. His name is Elisha," the man said, trembling with fear. "He is a man of God. He prays and the God of Israel reveals secrets to him. Then he goes to the King of Israel and tells him all things—even the secret things you whisper in your bedroom."

[Laughs.]

I can just see the king's face! Beat red with rage, fists shaking! "Go find out where he is," he ordered, "so I can send men and capture him!"

[He sobers as he tells the next part.]

My master—this same prophet, Elisha—and I were living in Dothan at the time. What they said was true about him. He had a relationship with the living God that I only barely glimpsed. Indeed, I was like a blind man.

The King of Aram sent horses and chariots and many men to Dothan, led by one of his generals. It did not take them long to locate our small home on the edge of the city and surround it. I remember hearing strange noises, like the waves of the sea, coming from the window above my bed. I rose and went to the door. When I saw the masses of Aramean soldiers, I fell to my knees in fear!

Elisha came up behind me, and I cried out to him, "Oh no, my lord! What shall we do?"

But Elisha just stood there for a moment surveying the scene. Then he patted my shoulder, as if to tell me to rise to my feet again, and said, "Do not be afraid. Those who are with us are more than those who are with them."

"What?" I asked. "But we are only two men!"

Then Elisha spoke again, but this time he was not speaking to me. "Open his eyes, LORD, so that he may see."

I looked again and saw a second army. But this army was of great men dressed in light and riding chariots of fire! They surrounded the house, filled the field and appeared amongst the Aramean army, before and behind and flanking the men on all sides! The Arameans did not know they were there, but my master and I saw them!

The Aramean general spotted us in the doorway. He lifted an arm to order his men to attack! This time, I did not fear.

Elisha prayed again. "LORD, God of Abraham, strike this army with blindness!"

The angelic hosts reached out and touched the men. Suddenly the army that was once charging toward us in an orderly fashion, began to falter. Horses and chariots crashed into one another. Men cried out in great distress, "I can't see! I can't see!" Others stumbled into the paths of oncoming chariots. Chaos reigned!

My master walked up to them and said in a loud voice, "Be still and hear me, men of Aram! This is not the road and this is not the city. Follow the sound of my voice, and I will lead you to the man you are looking for." Leaving their horses and chariots behind, the Arameans had no choice but to follow. Elisha led them to Samaria. Once there, Elisha prayed one more time. "LORD, open the eyes of these men so they can see." In that moment, the men regained their sight and saw they were trapped inside Samaria, surrounded by the men of Israel. When our king saw them, he asked Elisha, "Shall I kill them?"

"Do not kill them," Elisha answered. "Would you kill those you have captured with your own sword or bow? Set food and water before them so that they may eat and drink and then go back to their master." So, instead of death, the Aramean army was given a great feast! My master, Elisha, chose to repay their hatred and bloodlust with mercy.

[Laughs again.]

After that, the king of Aram found it very difficult to convince his men to raid us again and, for a time, we both experienced peace. ...And so the LORD opened my eyes a second time—to show me the power of God's grace.

[EXIT SERVANT]

THE END

❧ Section TWO ❧

Christian Living

Discovering God's Will: Part I

Scene:
Used Car Lot. The audience is the car lot.

Time Duration:
3-5 Minutes

Characters:
USED CAR SALESMAN: Used Car Salesman. Wears plaid pants and a sweater-vest.

BILL: Hyper-Christian car shopper.

Script:

[ENTER SALESMAN. ENTER BILL.]

SALESMAN
Hello, and welcome to Honest Abe's Used Cars! All the cars on this lot have been inspected by a mechanic and given a thorough cleaning and detailing!
[Wagging finger in air.]
If you can smell 'em, we don't sell 'em! How can I help you today?

BILL
Hi, I'm here looking for the car that God wants for me.

SALESMAN
The car that God wants for you... hmmm... I don't think I've ever heard that request before. Could you be a little more specific?

BILL
No, not really. The Bible doesn't say much about transportation, but I know that if I want to remain in God's will for my life, I can't take big decisions like this one lightly. God must know exactly which car would be perfect for me. I just need you to help me find it.

SALESMAN

Uhhhh… let me see.
[Surveys his lot while scratching his chin.]
That sounds a little *vague* to me…
[Laughing.]
hey, how about the Mitsubishi *Mirage*!
[Sweeps fingers wide at last word.]

BILL

[Not laughing.]
Look, Satan wants nothing better than to see me drive off this lot in the wrong car. But I'm determined to teach him a lesson by finding the very car God wants me to have!

SALESMAN

Then, how about the Dodge *Avenger*?
[Curls his hand into a fist at the last word in a wide motion.]

BILL

Very funny. No. I need something that will help me be a witness to those around me… something that will leave an impression on the generations that follow when they think of me.

SALESMAN

Ah! I have the perfect car for that! The Subaru *Legacy*!

BILL

Hmmm… Tempting… but I also want something that will remind me that God is central in my life and that I need to follow Him even when no one's looking.

SALESMAN

Let me think… Ah! The Acura *Integra*!

BILL

Now, I don't know….

SALESMAN

[Tiring.]
How about the Ford *Focus*! …Or, the Honda *Insight*!

[Emphasizes the model names.]

BILL

No... no....

SALESMAN

[Upset.]
I know! The Suzuki *Swift*!

BILL

Be patient. I'm waiting for that little "holy hunch" that will tell me which car to choose. I'm waiting for God to speak.
[Closes eyes and stretches arms out to the side with palms toward Heaven.]

SALESMAN

[Interrupts BILL's reverie.]
Well, you let me know when He does! Because right now I'm thinking the best car for you is the *Infiniti*!
[Large arm motions showing aggravation on last word. Stomps off. EXIT.]

BILL

Hey! Where are you going?
[Shrugs and then continues with his eyes closed and arms out for a moment. Then EXITS.]

TO BE CONTINUED...

Discovering God's Will: Part II

Setting:
A church classroom.

Props:
Duster
Cleaning Rag
Bike

Time Duration:
2-3 minutes

Characters:
BILL: Hyper Christian

JOE: Bible study leader.

DEMON: Dressed all in black and prances and sneaks around.

Script:

[ENTER JOE and DEMON. JOE is on stage dusting. DEMON hides behind the piano.]

JOE
[Pauses from dusting to look at his watch.]
Where is that guy?

[ENTER BILL, pushing a bike. JOE looks up and notices.]

Hey, Bill…. Weren't you going to buy a car this weekend?

BILL
[Looking depressed.]
Well… I went to the used car lot, but I just couldn't decide. I had some trouble figuring out which car God wanted for me, so I guess I'm stuck with my bike for now. Sorry I'm late.

JOE

Well, I'm sorry you had so much trouble, but I'm glad you finally made it. Look, we don't have much time. The others will be here soon and we still need to get this place ready.

[Hands BILL a cloth.]

DEMON

[Sneaks out from behind piano and begins to circle the men. She shakes her hands in front of their faces but they don't see her.]

BILL

[Starts to help wiping items down. DEMON approaches him.]
You know, Joe, I'm not sure I feel right about this.

JOE

What do you mean?

DEMON

[Is actively pestering BILL.]

BILL

Well, we're having a Bible study for people who have never been to church before—some of whom have been deeply involved in other religions. What if something goes wrong?

JOE

Well, I thought it was a good sign that they even agreed to come.

DEMON

[Sneers at JOE. Returns efforts to tormenting BILL.]

BILL

I did, too, at first... but now it seems so hard. What if we don't say the right thing? What if we accidentally chase them off? What if they start... start...

[Looks around to make sure no one's listening, scandalized by what he's about to say.]
cussing in church? I just wouldn't know what to do! This just doesn't feel right!

JOE
Well, how is it supposed to feel?

BILL
Well, for one, I thought I'd have peace about being involved in this ministry. But now all I feel is afraid and wary. I think maybe I'm not supposed to be here.

[Puts down cloth.]

JOE
Why don't we just stop and pray about this?

BILL
I have, Joe. I've prayed and I've prayed. I still feel uncomfortable. I keep waiting to have peace about the decision to involve myself in this ministry, and it hasn't come. I'm sorry. I have to go.

[BILL goes to get his bike and leaves.]

JOE
[Calling after him.]
Wait, Bill! This is a spiritual battlefield. You're not always going to feel at peace. Hey, come back!
[Runs after him. Exit JOE.]

DEMON
[Dances in victory. Exit.]

TO BE CONTINUED...

Discovering God's Will: Part III

Setting:
Bill's living room.

Props:
Fishing pole
Scroll
Chair

Time Duration:
2-3 minutes

Characters:

BILL: Hyper Christian who is searching.

STAGE HAND: Stays out of scene as much as possible.

Script:

BILL
> [Comes on stage looking very discouraged. Sighs loudly and sits. He begins to pray.]

Dear Lord, I've felt so confused lately! I feel like I've been running after You, and all You've been doing is running the other way! Like at the used car lot—I just wanted You to show me which car was the right one for me! And at the church outreach ministry—I was so confused by all these conflicting emotions that I didn't know what to do. And now I just feel like I'm letting everyone down, including You.

> [Sighs again.]

Lord, I really need to know what You want of me, and I need You to show me in a way that I'll understand. Obviously, I'm too dense to get it if You're being subtle. So... I have an idea. If you could just write down everything I'm supposed to do and send it to me, that would be great! Please, God? Won't you just send me a scroll from Heaven with Your exact instructions? OK... I'll wait.

[From behind something STAGE HAND lowers a scroll by use of a fishing pole until it dangles right in front of his eyes.]

BILL

Oh, wow, God! I can't believe You actually did it! Thank you!

[Excitedly removes the scroll and eagerly opens it.]

This is great! Now I'll know exactly what You want, and I'll be able to follow it to the letter!

[His countenance changes when he gets the scroll open. He is obviously disappointed. Head and shoulders droop. Wags the scroll in the air.]

Very funny, God! Very funny! I asked for a scroll from Heaven—and that's just what I got.

[Whining.]

I just didn't expect it to be in ancient Hebrew!

[Exit BILL carrying scroll and STAGE HAND.]

TO BE CONTINUED…

Discovering God's Will: Part IV

Setting:
Bill's living room.

Props:
Phone
A piece of paper with typing on it inside a yellow envelope.

Time Duration:
2-3 minutes

Characters:
BILL: Christian who is searching.

Script:

[Scene opens with BILL CENTER STAGE talking on phone, holding envelope.]

BILL
Yes, Dr. Wise, thank you for calling.
[Pause.]
Yes. It must have arrived today while I was out. I've got it right here, still in the envelope.
[Pause.]
Don't worry. The check is in the mail.
[Pause.]
Of course the check is good!
[Pause.]
Alright, then.
[Pause.]
Thanks.
[Hangs up.]
Finally! The translation of the scroll! The words God Himself sent to me so I could know His will for my life! I can hardly wait!
[Excitedly, opens envelope to read the paper.]
"For I know the plans I have for you," declares the Lord, "plans to prosper you and not to harm you, plans to give you hope and a future. Then you will call upon

me and come and pray to me, and I will listen to you. You will seek me and find me when you seek me with all your heart."

Wait a second.... I've heard this before. This is in the Bible already! That's in Jeremiah! So, I spent three hundred dollars to have a portion of Scripture translated that I already had?

[Drops head in hands for a moment.]

Great!

[Pause. Sighs and looks at it again.]

So what does this mean? Hmmm... Maybe God is less interested in what kind of car I drive than He is in... my love for Him. ...And, maybe God's promises that He has my best at heart and that my future is in His hands are more important than how I feel.

[Rereads]

"You will seek me and find me when you seek me with all your heart."

Hmmm... Can it really be that simple?

[Exit BILL.]

THE END

THE FASTEST TONGUE IN THE WEST

Topic: This is a comic skit about the evils of using your words to insult or tear down others.

Setting: A western town, on the street.

Key Verse: Ephesians 4:29 "Do not let any unwholesome talk come out of your mouths, but only what is helpful for building others up according to their needs, that it may benefit those who listen."

Props: A set of shutters and/or a newspaper (if extras are needed), broom, chair, advertisement, books.

Time Duration:
8-10 minutes

Characters:
NARRATOR

WHISTLER

WILL WILEY or GABBY GABBS (a.k.a. The Fastest Tongue in the West)

THE TOWN BARBER

THE TOWN DRESSMAKER

THE SCHOOL TEACHER

THE NEWCOMER.

EXTRAS: (Optional.) Someone to hide behind a newspaper and someone to run away as he comes, jump behind shutters and close them tight, and the whistler.)

Script:

> [ENTER BARBER with broom, DRESSMAKER with advertisement, TEACHER with books & NEWCOMER. All take positions and freeze in place while narration begins. SOUND of western whistling.]

NARRATOR

It was a regular little town—one of many that rested out on those wild western plains—where dreams came only in extra-large; and the only thing bigger was the hearts of the townsfolk. At least, that's how it was 'til ol' Will Wiley came to town and set up permanent residence as the meanest man in them parts. Most folks steered clear of him when they could, but few could escape an attack by Will—best known as *the fastest tongue in the west*!

> [ENTER WILL stage left. He starts to saunter slowly across the stage toward the BARBER. If EXTRAS are needed, one hides behind a newspaper and the other runs to the shutters and shuts herself/himself behind them.]

Yes! He was a fearsome thing to behold! He excelled at the art of the insult, the put-down, the affront, slights, slurs, zingers, and zappers! Verbal abuses of every kind and flavor slid from that forked tongue faster than a fox with lighted tail. And on this particular morning he was feeling the need for offensive speed. He just happened to first come across the town barber, who had just stepped out of his shop to sweep off his porch.

> [BARBER starts to sweep, seemingly oblivious to WILL at first, but then notices him and looks worried.]

Will saw his opportunity. He sauntered on up to the barber and, in the blink of an eye, said:

WILL

Do you cut your own hair or do you let a blind guy with a dull machete do it for you?

BARBER
[Drops broom and clutches his chest in agony.]
AH! You got me!
[Falls down to the ground as if dead.]

NARRATOR
And so The Fastest Tongue in the West walked a little taller.

[WILL smiles with pride and straightens up his shoulders and swaggers on toward the dressmaker.]

It so happened that Will saw the town dressmaker coming from her shop to pin up an advertisement for a very good deal on her latest styles.

[DRESSMAKER admires her advertisement for a while and then is about to pin it up when she sees WILL. She looks nervous but opens her mouth to greet him.]

But before she could even speak a single word, the Fastest Tongue in the West struck again!

WILL
That is the *ugliest* dress I've ever seen in my life!

[DRESSMAKER drops advertisement, clutches stomach and drops to her knees gasping for breath.]

And your shoes look like last season rejects!

[DRESSMAKER falls to the ground as if dead.]

NARRATOR
And The Fastest Tongue in the West walked a little taller.

[WILL begins to swagger toward the TEACHER.]

By the time Will saw the school teacher walking home from the school house with an armload of books, he was feeling mighty impressed with himself, but he still had plenty of ammunition left in his arsenal of insults. So, as she approached, he quickly shot off another one.

WILL

The only people more brainless than you are the people who hired you!

TEACHER

[Clutches shoulder in pain and stammers.]
I... I don't understand....

WILL

No, you wouldn't, would you?

[TEACHER clutches stomach, groans and falls to the ground as if dead.]

NARRATOR

And The Fastest Tongue in the West walked a little taller. Overall, Will felt it had been a pretty good day. No one had even come close to matching him with wit, speed, or ruthlessness. But as he came to the end of the road, Will saw a newcomer—someone he'd never insulted before. And he immediately thought of a perfect finish for a perfect day—one last conquest! So, oozing with confidence, The Fastest Tongue in the West swaggered right up to the newcomer and let fly one of his best zingers!

WILL

You look like a gremlin!

NARRATOR

But to Will's amazement, the newcomer didn't seem the least bit bothered by his comment. Hmmm.... Well, perhaps she hadn't heard him. He decided to try again.

WILL

You smell like stinky rotten eggs.

NARRATOR

But again, the newcomer seemed completely unaffected. In fact, she seemed rather amused. And *that* made Will mad! He decided this called for extreme measures! So, he dug deep and came up with his best insult yet—a sure thing—an insult that had never before failed him! Without mercy, he let it fly!

WILL

No one in this town likes you! They'll *never* like you! And, you'll *never* have any friends!

NARRATOR

Well, surely that would do the trick! But, to Will's utter horror, the newcomer just smiled!

[NEWCOMER smiles kindly at WILL and WILL is very disturbed and confused.]

How could this be? Why was she not rolling in agony in the dust? Was she somehow immune to his wicked words? Will was astounded! Mortified! And, worst of all, completely humiliated! Never before had anyone been able to withstand his vicious tongue! What if the townsfolk heard of this? He would be a laughing stock! His reign of terror would be over! …And for the first time, Will didn't know what to do. So, feeling he had nothing left to lose, he decided to find out what was going on.

WILL

Why aren't you bothered by anything I say?

NEWCOMER

Well, there is only one Voice I listen to when it comes to understanding who I am and what I'm worth.

WILL

And who's voice is that?

NEWCOMER

God's. See, God made me and so only He can tell me what I'm worth.

WILL

And what did He say?

NEWCOMER

He said that He loves me with an everlasting love and that I am His prized possession, and then He proved it by dying for all my sins so I could go live with Him in Heaven one day!

WILL

All that?

NEWCOMER

And more! ...In fact, He had some things to say about you, too.

WILL

Really?

NARRATOR

And, so, the newcomer ended up spending the entire night telling Will all about God, His love, and His sacrifice. And for the first time, The Fastest Tongue in the West had the biggest ears in the west. He was amazed by all he heard and more than anything, he wanted to experience that kind of love and forgiveness! By the time those western roosters crowed the next morning, Will felt like a changed man! But was he?

[TEACHER, DRESSMAKER & BARBER are sitting and rubbing their wounds. WILL mimes a goodbye with newcomer, smiles broadly and starts to head back through town.]

Will decided to return to his ranch to catch up on some sleep, but as he walked back through town, he came across the school teacher.

[TEACHER cowers in fear when she sees him coming.]

Seeing how hurt she looked, Will noticed a hard lump in his chest. It was a feeling he hadn't felt in a long time! What could it be? And then he realized what it was. Compassion. Regret. Empathy. So, for the first time in a long time, The Fastest Tongue in the West, used his quick tongue in a new way.

WILL

Hey, I'm sorry for what I said before. You're actually a very smart person, and I think the children of our town are lucky to have you for a teacher.

TEACHER

[Amazed and smiling.]
Wow! Well, thank you very much!

WILL

Jesus loves you. Goodbye!

[TEACHER freezes in place, smiling after him as WILL continues on toward the DRESSMAKER.]

NARRATOR

As Will continued on, he was amazed at how good it felt to say such a simple thing. And The Fastest Tongue in the West Walked a little taller. Next he saw the town dressmaker, still looking dazed from their earlier encounter. Perhaps his quick tongue could be used in this situation as well.

WILL

I'm sorry I said you had on an ugly dress. It's actually quite attractive, as are all the clothes in your shop. Jesus loves you, and I hope you'll let me show you that I can learn how to love people, too.

DRESSMAKER

Why, sure!

WILL

Maybe I'll come by later and you can help me pick out a new outfit.

DRESSMAKER

I'd be happy to!

[DRESSMAKER freezes in place, smiling after him as WILL continues on toward the BARBER.]

NARRATOR

And The Fastest Tongue in the West walked a little taller. Next he saw the Barber and he wasted no time at all. He let another blessing fly!

WILL

God loves you, Sir. And I hope you'll do me the favor of giving me a new haircut. I'd like my hair to look as good as yours does.

BARBER

Well, I'll be! Alright, then! Have a seat.

[WILL sits down and barber pretends to cut his hair.]

NARRATOR

And The Fastest Tongue in the West walked a little—well, actually, he was shorter because he was sitting down—but he *felt* taller, and from that day forward he made sure never again to utter curses, but only blessings on all he met—because, only God can tell anyone what they are really worth. And to God we are each worth the very life of His only Son, Jesus Christ.

[SOUND of western whistling.]

THE END

The Living and the Dead

Setting: A small church, shown by several chairs set up opposite a small podium. Preacher is standing behind podium. Most of the chairs are full by people who have gone completely limp. Some are lying in the ground as if dead. He's preaching.

Time Duration:
4-7 minutes

Characters:
PREACHER

ALLISON

A BUNCH OF DEAD PEOPLE

Script:

[ENTER ALLISON. She looks around, confused, but finds a chair. As she sits, the limp arm of the guy next to her fall on her shoulder or across her lap. She is a bit weirded out, but leaves it there and begins to listen to the PREACHER.]

PREACHER
[Holding Bible open to appropriate passage.]
And so, my brothers, Ephesians 2 says, "As for you, you were dead in your transgressions and sins, in which you used to live when you followed the ways of this world and of the ruler of the kingdom of the air, the spirit who is now at work in those who are disobedient. All of us also lived among them at one time, gratifying the cravings of our sinful nature and following its desires and thoughts. Like the rest, we were by nature objects of wrath. But because of his great love for us, God, who is rich in mercy, made us alive with Christ even when we were dead in transgressions—it is by grace you have been saved."

ALLISON
[Waves hand in the air to get his attention.]
Excuse me?

PREACHER

Uh, yes?

ALLISON

I'm very sorry to interrupt, but what's wrong with all these people?

PREACHER

[Matter-of-factly.]
Oh, well, they're dead.

ALLISON

What? EEEEEWW!
[Disgusted and lifts up the limp arm of the guy next to her and tries to get it out of her way.]
What do you mean, 'they're dead?' Didn't you just get finished saying that they were made alive in Christ?

PREACHER

Oh, right, well. I guess, technically they're "alive in Christ."
[Makes quotes with fingers.]
But haven't you ever heard of a dead church?

ALLISON

Um, I think so.

PREACHER

Well, you're in it.
[Looks back at the Bible.]
Let's see, where was I?

ALLISON

Wait just a minute! I don't get it! How can they be dead if they're alive?

PREACHER

Well, they're not fully dead... I don't think. Actually, I'm not sure. See, it's been a long time since I've detected movement out there.

ALLISON

When was the last time?

PREACHER

Oh, well, we had the band Family Force Five come through here a few years ago! Now there's a band that'll get your heart pumping! Some of these folks got a little jittery. I even detected a pulse in that guy over there for a while. ...But then the band moved on to their next show and everything just quieted down again.

ALLISON

So, you just keep preaching? What for?

PREACHER

Well, I keep hoping things will change. I'll preach a good sermon and I might see an ear twitch or a toe wiggle. I'll get excited for a while, but then nothing ever happens. I'm beginning to think that my preaching alone just isn't going to do it.

ALLISON

So, what happened to start this... this... epidemic?

PREACHER

Oh, you mean the spiritual death that seems to spread like wild fire?

ALLISON

[Alarmed, covers her nose and mouth with her hand so as not to catch it.]
Uh, huh.

PREACHER

Well, it started the usual way—people forgetting how much Jesus loves them—just because they're His. So, then they started looking for love from others. That turned to unhealthy relationships, lies, distrust, gossip, slander—you name it. Eventually, they stopped hearing me altogether. First their hearing went, then their sight, and finally they just fell over, and that's where they've been ever since.
[Motioning to those on the ground and slumped in their chairs.]

ALLISON

And what about you?

PREACHER

Well, I just keep preaching… and hoping.
[Frowning.]

ALLISON

Why bother?

PREACHER

I'm not sure, really….
[Puts down his Bible on the podium.]

ALLISON

[Approaches the preacher.]
Look, I don't think preaching is what they need right now. I think they need Christ—they need to remember how much Jesus loves them—just for who they are! Just because they're His!

PREACHER

Well, but if I don't preach, then what will I do?

ALLISON

You can still preach. But first, I think we should pray. Because, even you said you don't think preaching alone is going to do it.

PREACHER

Well, that sounds like a good idea. Would you be willing to pray with me?

ALLISON

Sure!

[ALLISON and PREACHER sit down together and mime praying. Slowly, there is movement detected in dead crowd. Eventually one of them wakes up, stretches and yawns as if waking from a long sleep. Allison and Preacher smile, hug him and ask him to join in the prayer, which he does. Soon, others are welcomed and join in the prayer until the whole church is praying together. Then the preacher joyfully reads from the Bible.]

PREACHER

Romans 6:11-14 "In the same way, count yourselves dead to sin but alive to God in Christ Jesus. Therefore do not let sin reign in your mortal body so that you obey its evil desires. Do not offer the parts of your body to sin, as instruments of wickedness, but rather offer yourselves to God, as those who have been brought from death to life; and offer the parts of your body to him as instruments of righteousness. For sin shall not be your master, because you are not under law, but under grace."

THE END

The Other Side of the Room

Setting:
A church Sanctuary. Make stage look like a sanctuary—a pulpit STAGE LEFT with a series of chairs in before it, STAGE RIGHT. It should be set up so that we're looking at it as if from the side of the room, not from the front or the back.

Props:
Bible

Time Duration:
2-3 minutes

Characters:
PASTOR   Dressed nicely.
BRENT   Holds a Bible and sits in the front row.
ALICIA   Sits in the second row, right behind BRENT.
STRANGER   Sits in the back row, alone.
EXTRAS

Script:

[Scene opens with PASTOR behind the pulpit and the rest of characters in seats.]

PASTOR
OK, and now it's time for our meet and greet! Why don't you say hello to someone new today?

[EXTRAS start pretending to greet one another, shaking hands, etc. No one talks to STRANGER.]

BRENT
[Turning around and shaking ALICIA'S hand.]
Hi, Alicia! Great to see you today!

ALICIA

Hi, Brent! Hey, how's your fundraising for that Africa mission trip going?

BRENT

Oh, it's going great! The money is coming in, my visa arrived this week, and I already have enough for my plane tickets! God is good!

ALICIA

That's wonderful, Brent! I just love seeing how the Lord provides.

BRENT

Me, too! I'm so excited to go meet people who need the love of Jesus in their lives! To reach out and shake their hands! To really get to know them, and share the love Jesus has given to me.

ALICIA

Wonderful, Brent! That's so great to hear. And, hey! Guess what? You can get some practice this very morning! Look!
    [Motions to STRANGER.]
That girl is new today. Looks like she could use a friend, too.

BRENT

Oh, well, I… I don't know….

ALICIA

What's the matter?

BRENT

Well, she wouldn't know who I am, and…

ALICIA

The people in Africa don't know who you are.

BRENT

But, that's different. They expect people to come talk to them about Jesus.

ALICIA

Well, I doubt this girl would show up in church if she didn't expect that, too.

BRENT

But, what if I come off too pushy? I might turn her off.

ALICIA

Well, I'd bet that having people in church refuse to look her in the eye is an even bigger turn-off.

BRENT

True, but she's way back there on the other side of the room. It would be weird for me to go all that way. Besides, the people around her are supposed to do that. I would be stealing their blessing.

ALICIA

Doesn't look like anyone's being "blessed" this morning. And how can you be willing to cross an ocean to share God's love, but not the room?

BRENT

Well, it's just that…

[PASTOR returns to pulpit and raises his hands. People start returning to their places.]

BRENT

Oh, hey. The pastor's ready to start again.

[ALICIA, incensed, grabs her purse and starts to leave the aisle.]

BRENT

Hey, where are you going?

ALICIA

To steal your blessing.

[ALICIA heads to the back of the church and sits down next to STRANGER, smiling and shaking her hand. EXIT ALL.]

THE END

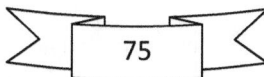

75

❧ SECTION THREE ❧

Evangelistic Skits

Blowing Away the Stereotypes

Setting:
Stage left is just outside a coffee shop. Stage right is inside the coffee shop where there are two chairs and a table set up near a coffee vendor's booth. The coffee vendor is behind the booth, cleaning glasses and waiting for customers. There is a sign in front of her booth reading: FANCY COFFEE, $6.00.

Props:
Table
Two Chairs
Coffee Mugs
Sign: FANCY COFFEE $6.00
Signs (See descriptions below.)

Time Duration:
8-10 minutes

Characters

JACK:　　　　Wears a series of signs around his neck, one behind the other, in the following order with the first one showing: SEEKER, SKEPTIC, ATHEIST, SEEKER.

ALLAN:　　　Wears a sign around his neck that reads: ATHIEST.

MAXINE:　　Wears a series of signs around his neck, one behind the other, in the following order with the first one showing: CHRISTIAN, JUDGER.

STEVE:　　　Wears a series of signs around his neck, one behind the other, in the following order with the first one showing: CHRISTIAN, HYPOCRITE.

CHRISTIAN:　Wears a series of signs around his neck, one behind the other, in the following order with the first one showing: CHRISTIAN, JESUS.

PRETTY GIRL

EXTRAS: Three or four coffee shop customers.

Script:

[Scene opens with EXTRAS on stage. They are buying coffee, milling about with mugs in their hands miming casual conversation, or sitting reading books. ENTER JACK with a sign around his neck that reads: SEEKER, and ALLAN with a sign around his neck that reads: ATHEIST.]

ALLAN

It looks crowded in there… as usual.

JACK

The best places always are.

ALLAN

I think I'll find another place this morning.

JACK

Well, see ya at work.

ALLAN

[Turns to go, but then turns back with a last remark.]
And watch out for the Christians in there. They like to try to corner you into their obnoxious little conversations. They're all just judgers and hypocrites. Just keep your distance if you know what's good for you.

JACK

Thanks…. I'll keep that in mind.

[EXIT ALLAN and JACK enters coffee shop. He buys a coffee and sits down in one of the empty chairs. ENTER MAXINE wearing a sign around her neck that reads: CHRISTIAN. MAXINE buys a coffee and then can't seem to find a place to sit. She approaches JACK.]

MAX

This seat taken? It's pretty crowded in here today.

JACK

Best places always are. Help yourself.

MAXINE

[Sits with an appreciative smile.]
Thanks! Hi, my name's Maxine.

JACK

Jack.

[They shake hands.]

MAXINE

So, tell me a little about yourself, Jack.

JACK

Well, I just moved here a couple of months ago.

MAXINE

No, kidding! Welcome to Churchville!

JACK

Thanks.

MAXINE

What brought you here?

JACK

Actually, I came to be closer to my girlfriend.

MAXINE

[Suddenly suspicious.]
Oh, really?

JACK

That's right.
[Proudly and a bit self-conscious.]
It's getting pretty serious.

MAXINE

How serious?

JACK

Well, we moved in together when I got here, and things have been going real well so far.

MAXINE

[Snide.]
I'll bet!

JACK

What do you mean?

MAXINE

[Angrily.]
I mean, it must be nice to get whatever you want with no strings attached. You know, you should really marry the girl if she's as great as you say, instead of living in sin! You know what?
[Stands and rips off her sign to reveal another that reads: JUDGER.]
I've got to go! You obviously don't want to have anything to do with morality!
[Leaves her coffee on the table and storms out.]

[Coffee vendor comes and cleans up his mug. JACK is depressed. He stands up and paces uncomfortably for a while, and then tears off his sign, revealing another that reads: SKEPTIC. He returns to his seat to finish his coffee. STEVE, one of the other coffee drinkers approaches, wearing a sign that reads: CHRISTIAN.]

STEVE

Hey, I see your friend left. Do you mind if I sit?

JACK

Oh…. Uh, no. Go ahead.

STEVE

Thanks, buddy!

JACK

No problem.

STEVE

Hey, I couldn't help but overhear that girl. Don't worry about her. There's nothing wrong with what you're doing.

JACK

Well, thanks. So, I guess you're not a Christian, then?

STEVE

Oh, I'm a Christian, alright. I said the little prayer and everything. I just live my own brand of Christianity. See, I figure that if God is love, then what's wrong with spreading His love around a little bit?

JACK

Well, that seems to make sense, but—

STEVE

See, take me for instance. I'm just like you. I'm living with my girlfriend and still go to church. I just don't mention it around the wrong people, if you know what I mean. Ha! Ha!

JACK

So, does that work?

STEVE

[Frowns]
Uh... usually.

JACK

What do you mean, 'usually'?

STEVE

Well, it works when they don't find out, that is. See, I had this one girlfriend, Beth, who, as long as she didn't come with me to church, everything went fine. But then she started wanting to go along, and eventually the whole story came out. And then I was living with Lisa who happened to run into the pastor at the grocery store and got to talking! And then there was Alexis who—

JACK
Whoa! How many girls have you lived with?

STEVE
All of them.

JACK
But don't you believe the Bible's teachings are true?

STEVE
Mostly, I guess.

[PRETTY GIRL walks by and he focuses on her.]

STEVE
Oh, hold on a minute, buddy! I'll have to catch you later! I've never seen *her* in here before!
[Jumps up, rips off his sign to reveal one that reads: HYPOCRITE, and pursues PRETTY GIRL out of coffee shop and offstage.]

[Coffee vendor removes mug.]

JACK
[Angry and confused.]
What? This is ridiculous!
[Again he stands up, paces and tears off his sign to reveal another that reads: ATHEIST. Returns to seat, dejected.]

[Enter CHRISTIAN wearing a sign that reads: CHRISTIAN.]

CHRISTIAN
Hey. Do you mind some company?

JACK
[Still very angry and bitter.]
Well, I don't know. That depends!

CHRISTIAN
On what?

JACK

If you're a Christian or not.

CHRISTIAN

Actually, I am a Christian.

JACK

Well, then I doubt you'd want to sit here.

CHRISTIAN

[Looks at the chair curiously, as if to inspect it. Then, jokingly.]
Why, is the devil sitting in it already?

JACK

[Smirks.]
No… but you'll probably think the devil's sitting in this one.
[Motioning to his own.]

CHRISTIAN

Why would I think that?

JACK

Because I'm an atheist, that's why!

CHRISTIAN

Oh, is that all? Well, if you don't mind, I'd love to join you, Atheist…
or do you go by another name?
[Smiles and sits.]

JACK

[Relaxes a bit and gives a small smile.]
It's Jack, actually.

CHRISTIAN

Nice to meet you, Jack.
[They shake hands.]
Now, what's all this trouble about Christians?

JACK

Well, the first guy told me I was living in sin for living with my girlfriend, and the next one seemed like all he did was use women! I just can't figure you Christians out! And if what I've seen so far is what it means to be a Christian, I don't want to be one!

CHRISTIAN

[Considers his words for a moment.]
I'm sorry, Jack. I'm sorry Christ's followers have misrepresented Him to you.

JACK

You know what? Don't even worry about it. I've given up on the whole thing, anyway.

CHRISTIAN

That's too bad. You see, before I knew Christ, I was very much like you. I was sure Christians were nothing but judgers and hypocrites. And, I'm sad to say, some of them are. But, if we judge Christ only by His followers, we end up missing the real message. If you want to know about Jesus, shouldn't you go straight to the source? Find out who He is? What He said? What He did?

JACK

Maybe… but I'm just tired of the whole thing! It's just too late!

CHRISTIAN

Well, sorry about that. Thanks for letting me share your table, Jack.
[Stands to go, but then turns back to JACK.]
Say, I'm about to have a little Bar-B-Q at my place just around the corner from here. Would you like to join me?

JACK

Even though I'm an atheist?

CHRISTIAN

Sure, why not?

JACK

Well… I guess so. That could be fun.

[Smiles and stands up to follow him.]

[CHRISTIAN takes his mug back to the counter and then turns to audience and tears off his sign to reveal one that reads: JESUS. He walks toward the exit and waits for JACK to follow.]

CHRISTIAN
Course, I have to warn you. It might be a bit crowded.

JACK
Well, the best places always are.
[JACK faces the audience and tears off his sign to reveal one that reads: SEEKER. Then, he follows CHRISTIAN out.]

[Exit ALL.]

THE END

Everyman

Special Effects:
"Amazing Grace" partial music.
Lights need to flicker on and off.

Props:
Doors with a sign above them that reads: CHURCH
Scythe
Black, hooded robe
Fake paper money
Bottle caps in bags or pocket of MONEY
Large dictionary
Baby doll
Bowl of chips
Beer or wine bottle
Several magazines
Nerd glasses with tape
Dark sunglasses
Handkerchief
Funnel
Bowl of Food

Time Duration:
15-20 minutes

Characters:

EVERYMAN: Regular guy, dressed casually.

DEATH: Dressed in long, black, hooded robe and
                   carrying a scythe.

FRIEND: Another casually dressed girl or boy.

MONEY: Girl or boy dressed like a gambling bookie,
                   with a visor and lots of money sticking out of
                   his or her pockets. Sound of coins jingling
                   when he walks and he always is counting out

bills while he talks. He chews gum and talks with a Brooklyn accent.

KNOWLEGE: Girl who acts really dumb and klutzy. She carries a large dictionary.

GOOD DEEDS: A nurse carrying a baby doll wrapped up.

SELF-CONTROL: Fat guy (can actually be a skinny guy with his clothes stuffed with pillows) who carries a bowl of chips and has a bottle of alcohol under his arm and magazines stuffed in his pockets.

BEAUTY: A girl who wears thick glasses with tape on them and has her hair teased up all over the place. Her face is always scrunched up and she wears an ugly dress with one sock pulled all the way up and the other around her ankle. She chews gum and she talks in a squeaky voice.

STRENGTH: A wimp—dressed like a nerd with his pants pulled up to his chest and suspenders.

SIGHT: A blind girl or boy using a cane and wearing dark sunglasses. (No lines.)

SMELL: A girl or boy with a terrible cold who carries a handkerchief.

HEARING: A partially deaf boy (or girl) who uses a funnel in his ear when someone is speaking to him.

TOUCH: A boy or girl in a coma who gets carried in and out by the others. (No lines.)

TASTE: A boy or girl carrying a bowl of food who is always eating out of it. (No lines.)

DEMONS: Two girls or boys dressed in all black. (No lines.)

Script:

ACT I, SCENE I

Setting: City street corner in front of a church. Bus stop with bench nearby and bushes.

[ENTER STAGE LEFT EVERYMAN. He walks from left of stage to right, toward the church. He pauses in front of the church. "Amazing Grace" can be heard coming from inside.]

EVERYMAN

Wow! All those people in there—just wasting their time! They're resting their minds just like they're resting their rumps. Hah! Maybe they think they need all that spiritual garbage—as if they're going to die tomorrow! Some people spend *years* in church when they *could* be out having fun! …Maybe when I'm old and gray I'll step inside—but not until then! I've got too much *life* ahead of me!

[He continues walking past the church toward the bus stop. ENTER DEATH STAGE RIGHT.]

DEATH

Whoa, there! I believe you're the man I'm looking for!

EVERYMAN

I don't believe we've ever met. You must be mistaken, Sir.

[Starts to walk away but DEATH blocks him.]

DEATH

Oh, no! You're him alright! Your name is Everyman, correct?

EVERYMAN

[Hesitantly.]

Yes… and you are?

DEATH

A messenger! I've come from God to bring you to judgment. Perhaps you've heard of me. My name is Death!

EVERYMAN

Look, buddy, you sound like you've been smoking some pretty heavy stuff! ...Just say "no" okay?

[Starts to walk off but DEATH blocks him again.]

DEATH

I don't think you understand. Your time has come! ...But, perhaps you need a little convincing.

[He touches EVERYMAN on the shoulder. Immediately the lights dim and flicker. EVERYMAN clutches at his left arm and chest and falls to his knees crying out in pain.]

EVERYMAN

Ah! The pain! It's like my ...heart is going to burst!

DEATH

Close.

EVERYMAN

Who are you?

DEATH

I told you. I am Death—and you're coming with me!

EVERYMAN

OK! I believe you! ...Just give me a minute, will you?

[DEATH takes his hand away. The lights return to normal, and EVERYMAN rises to his feet, still breathing hard.]

DEATH

Are you ready to go?

EVERYMAN

What? Now? No! No, I'm not! Can't you just give me a few more years? Like say, about 50? 50 years isn't anything to you. By then I could have all my earthly accounts settled, and I could be religious and everything. I could—

DEATH

You got ten minutes.

EVERYMAN

Ten minutes? I don't even know where to begin! How about 30 years—that's 20 less than I asked for at first!

DEATH

[Looking at his watch.]
9 minutes, 53 seconds... 52... 51....

EVERYMAN

OK! OK! I've got to think! ...I've got it! I'll get all my friends to go with me to put in a good word for me with God. Yeah!
[Makes a quick call on his cell phone.]
Hi, Friend? Could you meet me at the bus stop immediately? ...Yeah!
...It's an emergency! Thanks!
[Hangs up.]

[ENTER FRIEND STAGE LEFT.]

FRIEND

Here I am!

EVERYMAN

Ah, Friend! I'm glad you're here! I'm in big trouble!

FRIEND

Anything for you, Everyman! What are friends for? I'll do anything I can, Ol' Buddy! Just name it! I'd go with you even unto Death!

EVERYMAN

Oh, I was hoping you'd say that!

FRIEND

Uh, ...say what?

EVERYMAN

That's exactly what I need! You see, I'm going to die any minute!
[Glances nervously at DEATH.]

FRIEND

Die?

EVERYMAN

Yeah, and I need someone to go with me, you know—to put in a good word for me with God. You've been with me for so long, I'm sure you'd know just what to say.

FRIEND

Hey, hey, hey! Hold on just one moment! I'm not going to go with you *this* time, Buddy! You're on your own!

EVERYMAN

What? But you said you'd go with me even unto Death!

FRIEND

Yeah, well, you never were very good in English class! You see, there's a difference, between an *expression* and the *literal*. This 'going with you till Death' thing was *definitely* an expression! Look, I gotta go! Good luck with God an' all. …You're going to need it!

[EXIT FRIEND STAGE LEFT.]

EVERYMAN
[Calling after FRIEND.]
How can you just leave me that way, after we've been together for so long? …Oh, Man! Now what? My only Friend is gone! …Now who can I turn to?

DEATH

What about Jesus?

EVERYMAN

Who?

DEATH

Oh, boy!

EVERYMAN

I know! My Money! Money has always been there for me!

[ENTER MONEY STAGE RIGHT, counting money.]

MONEY
You called, Master?

EVERYMAN
Yes, Money, I'm going to die soon—

MONEY
[Without feeling and still counting his money.]
Oh, that's a shame!

EVERYMAN
Yes, and I need you to come along with me to help me get into
Heaven. You know, a little bribe here and there. We could pay off
the angel Gabriel at the Gate—Oh, and whoever it is with that book!
…Uh …What's it called again? …*Jesus Had a Little Lamb*? Anyway,
then I won't have to spend eternity with this guy.
[Motions to DEATH, who looks mildly insulted.]

MONEY
Oh, no, Master. I cannot go with you!

EVERYMAN
What? What do you mean? You've always been there for me! I *own*
you!

MONEY
Actually, that's a common misconception.
[Chuckles until he sees that EVERYMAN is not amused and
then he gets serious.]
No one owns me! I was only a temporary companion to you. When
you leave, I'll go on to someone else. I follow *no* man to the grave!

EVERYMAN
How can this be? You tricked me! You, who I loved most of all!

MONEY
That was exactly your problem! You gave me the love you should've
given to God. Don't feel bad. Many men and women make the same

mistake. I have led many to Hell who thought they had already tasted Heaven!

EVERYMAN

Get away from me, you vile thing! How could I have trusted you?

[EXIT MONEY.]

DEATH

Time's up, Everyman! Let's go!

EVERYMAN

Wait! I have turned to my Friend and to my Money and both have deserted me in my time of greatest need! Now I only have myself! I know! I will ask my Knowledge to help me!

[ENTER KNOWLEDGE stage right. she trips and bumps into the bench, almost falling.]

DEATH

[Irritated.]
Oh, Great! Here we go again!

EVERYMAN

[Covers his face with one hand.]
Oh, no!

KNOWLEDGE

[To DEATH.]
You called?

EVERYMAN

Over here!

KNOWLEDGE

Oh!
[Giggles stupidly.]

EVERYMAN

Knowledge, I need you help me. You must convince God to allow me a place in Heaven.

KNOWLEDGE

[Pulls out a dictionary and starts thumbing through it.]
God... God... God... God...

EVERYMAN

This is hopeless!

DEATH

It seems that *God* wasn't a part of your vocabulary, Everyman.

KNOWLEDGE

[Still looking.]
OK, ummm, let's see. ...A, B, C, D...

EVERYMAN

I will call on my Good Deeds instead! Surely God will look favorable upon them!

[ENTER GOOD DEEDS.]

EVERYMAN

My Good Deeds is a nurse?

NURSE

Actually, Sir, this is Good Deeds.
[She motions to the baby in her arms.]

EVERYMAN

What?

DEATH

I guess 'Good Deeds' should be singular. Like, your *one* Good Deed!
[Laughs at his own joke.]

EVERYMAN

[Not amused. Angry and frustrated.]

I should've let that old lady find her own way across the street!

DEATH
[Sarcastically.]
Nice attitude!

EVERYMAN
[To KNOWLEDGE and GOOD DEEDS.]
Leave me! Neither of you could ever help me get into Heaven!

[EXIT GOOD DEEDS STAGE LEFT. KNOWLEDGE stays.]

KNOWLEDGE
Heaven!
[Thumbs through dictionary.]
Heaven… Heaven… Heaven…

EVERYMAN
I know! I will call on my Self-Control!

DEATH
Uh, bad idea…

[ENTER SELF-CONTROL STAGE LEFT.]

EVERYMAN
Uh, oh!

SELF-CONTROL
[Talks around a mouthful of chips.]
You called? I got a great new item for you, Everyman!
[Shows him the bottle.]
Check it out!

EVERYMAN
[Whispers angrily.]
Not in front of *him*!
[Motions to DEATH.]

DEATH
I heard that.

EVERYMAN
[To SELF-CONTROL]
You disgust me!

SELF-CONTROL
Hey! What's gotten into you? You've always appreciated the finer things in life!
[Holds up the bottle up again temptingly.]

EVERYMAN
Why aren't you stronger?

SELF-CONTROL
Hey! I can lift 15 cans of beer, 5 pizzas, and 6 bags of chips all in one sitting—and that's no lie! Check these babies out!
[Holds up a flabby arm.]

EVERYMAN
[Turning to DEATH.]
How could I have lived like this for so long? I pass by here every day!
[Motions to church.]
Every day I had a chance to step inside and learn about God. If I only had just opened that door—even once—I might've found out the truth! ...Now it's too late!

DEATH
Uh, speaking of late...
[Points to his watch.]
The hearse has been kept waiting for over 15 minutes now, and –

EVERYMAN
Wait! Just one more chance! I will call on my Strength, my Beauty, and my Five Senses!

[ENTER BEAUTY, STRENGTH, SIGHT, and TASTE STAGE RIGHT. HEARING and SMELL drag in TOUCH with them.]

BEAUTY

You called?

EVERYMAN

Who are you?

BEAUTY

I'm your Beauty! Couldn't you tell?

EVERYMAN

But everyone tells me what a good-lookin' guy I am!

BEAUTY

Hey! No need to get insulting! ...But, to be honest, I have looked better. However, with this guy around
[Motions to DEATH]
I get a little ...how should I put it? ... wind-blown.

DEATH

[Proudly.]
Ah, yes! The winds of Death easily blow Beauty away!

EVERYMAN

[Looks at STRENGTH.]
And you?

STRENGTH

I am Strength. I'm afraid the winds of death take their toll on me, too. No amount of working out can save me now.

DEATH

The Bible says that man's strength is only vanity.

KNOWLEDGE

[Thumbing through dictionary.]
Bible ...Bible ...Bible...

DEATH

It seems you could've done with a good vocabulary lesson!

EVERYMAN

Who are they?

DEATH

[Points them out.]
The blind one over there is Sight. Though you could see with your eyes, your spirit was blind to the things of God. That one is taste.

EVERYMAN

The one eating the chocolate-covered grasshoppers? Good grief! ...And him?

DEATH

The one in the coma? That's Touch.

EVERYMAN

Great! Just what I need! You, with the handkerchief! Who are you?

SMELL

I'm your sense of ...of ...ACHOO! Smell. Unfortunately, I've got a bit of a head cold... ACHOO!

EVERYMAN

And you? Who are you?

HEARING

Say what? We're going to the zoo? Wonderful! I *love* animals!

EVERYMAN

No! No! Who *are* you?

HEARING

We're going to the bar, too? Awesome!

DEATH

He is your Hearing. You have been deaf to God's voice for many years.

EVERYMAN

Who else can I call on? There must be someone else!

DEATH

There is no one.

EVERYMAN

You're a real downer, you know that?

DEATH

You did not call on the only One who could save you during your life—no one else can help you during your death.

EVERYMAN

But I'm not dead yet!

[As they speak EXIT KNOWLEDGE, STRENGTH, BEAUTY, SIGHT, and SMELL STAGE LEFT. TASTE and HEARING carry away TOUCH STAGE LEFT. ENTER DEMONS STAGE RIGHT at the same time. DEMONS begin creeping around EVERYMAN.]

EVERYMAN

[Frightened.]

Get away from me! There must be someone who can help me! Please! Give me a chance!

DEATH

You had many chances. You yourself said that you walked by this church every day. You always thought you could come to God later. And, sadly, what you were seeking most in life—acceptance, joy, and freedom—could only be found through those doors. But you had too much to do. I believe your exact words were, 'I've got too much *life* ahead of me.'

[DEMONS are getting closer and milling about him.]

I guess you were wrong.

[DEMONS seize EVERYMAN and begin dragging him off stage. He begins screaming.]

EVERYMAN

No! No! Please! Just give me another chance! Pleeeeeese!

[EXIT ALL.]

ACT I, SCENE II

[EVERYMAN is in bed far left stage. he wakes up with a start and screams.]

EVERYMAN

Ahhh! No! No! -- Huh? Where am I? ... It was only a dream! ...What a horrible nightmare!

[Gets up and shakes the sleep off. Looks at clock.]

Oh, man, I'm late! I've gotta get to work!

[He throws a suit coat over his pjs and runs out the door. He walks down the street by the church. ENTER DEATH dressed in normal clothes. Their eyes meet. DEATH tips his hat to EVERYMAN. EVERYMAN halts in his steps, pauses, looks back at the church, looks at DEATH again, and then turns and bolts inside the church. DEATH looks very puzzled. EXIT DEATH.]

THE END

HADES COMPLAINT DEPARTMENT

Scene:

Stage is set up with a row of chairs at left stage and a desk (or table) and chair at right. On the desk are some in/out files, a phone, a clipboard with a large amount of paper clipped in it with the top looking like a sign-in sheet of some kind, a pencil, a long, thin piece of paper with a long number on it and several loose sheets of paper. A large sign reading: "HADES COMPLAINT DEPARTMENT" is in a visible location. (Use more than one sign, if necessary.) The stage is in shadow and lights are centered on two people walking along the front of the stage at ground level.

Time Duration:

15-20 minutes

Characters:

CHRIS: A young skeptic.

REBECCA: CHRIS'S friend, who is trying to witness to him.

CLERK: The clerk with an attitude who runs the desk at the Hades Complaint Department. Chews gum and uses a nail file.

OG-DUG: Client Number 2. He is a caveman. He has several small sticks in his hands.

BENNY: A client. He's a scruffy teenager who looks like a trouble-maker. He has no lines, but can pretend to do air guitar from time to time and can be wearing an IPod.

MARGARET: A woman wearing a business suit. She has a magazine with her.

KING SAUL: Character from the Bible, wearing appropriate garb. He has no lines.

EXTRAS: There can be several extra characters from various countries and time periods filling some of the seats in the waiting area.

Script:

LIGHTS CENTER ON STAGE

[ENTER REBECCA and CHRIS, coming from stage right and heading toward stage left. CHRIS is carrying a small stack of papers.]

REBECCA
So, Chris, what did you think of church this morning?

CHRIS
Honestly, Rebecca... I mean, I don't want to hurt your feelings 'cause I know you believe in all of that, but I just don't buy it.

REBECCA
Buy what?

CHRIS
You know... that Jesus is the *only* way to getting right with God. I think churches just tell you that so they won't have to compete with other churches for your money.

REBECCA
[Feeling annoyed and insulted.]
Nice.

CHRIS
I'm sorry. It's just that why would God make only ONE way, when there are SO many different kinds of people out there? And I've read into the other religions. They sound okay. Why not just let people find God the best way they can?

REBECCA
Well, because---

CHRIS

[Glances at his watch and interrupts.]
Oh, no! I'm late! Look, we can talk about this later! I've gotta run!

[CHRIS runs down small alley behind the stage . Suddenly, he slips. His papers go flying and his feet come up. We hear an "ugh" and then silence. During the silence the rest of the characters take their places on stage. When they are settled, the lights come on and CHRIS stumbles through center stage back opening, rubbing his head.]

CLERK

[Talking on the phone with feet up on the desk and chewing gum.]
OK.... OK.... OK, Sheila, I'll check.
[Covers phone with one hand and yells.]
Benny! Benny Raymond, are you here?

BENNY

[Waves at her from his seat.]

CLERK

[Back on the phone.]
Yes, Sheila, he's here.... Sorry about that.... Well, you know, you just can't use fishing line as a bungee cord. It's just not safe.... It's the testosterone, Sheila. It makes men crazy until they're about 35.... How do I know? We get plenty of doctors coming through here, you know. Of course, not so many as lawyers. I can't tell you HOW many times I've had to explain that you just can't sue the devil!
[Notices CHRIS.]
Oh! Sorry, Sheila. It seems I've got another client. OK. Bye.
[HANGS UP PHONE, sits up straight and looks at CHRIS.]
You, there. Do you have some sort of complaint?

CHRIS

[Confused and disoriented.]
What?

CLERK

[Annoyed and pronouncing her words loudly and slowly.]

Do You Have A COMPLAINT?

CHRIS

Where am I?

CLERK

[Sighs loudly and mutters under her breath.]
Great! Here we go again!
[To CHRIS.]
You are in Hades, Sir—in the Complaint Department. Do you have a complaint?

CHRIS

Wait a minute! Am I dead?

CLERK

[Sarcastic.]
Well, now, I've ONLY been here for about ten millennia, but in my LIMITED experience, live people don't usually show up in Hades, now do they? Are you going to file a complaint, or what?

CHRIS

[Recovering and approaching the desk.]
Uh, yeah. Yeah, I am. See, I was just walking along and I slipped. I mean, people don't DIE from slipping, do they? Isn't that a little unfair! What about—

CLERK

[Holds up her hands.]
Whoa! Hold on there, Buster! Save it for the complaint forms.
[Hands him clipboard.]
Here, take a number and fill this out. You got your registration page, Complaint Form 209, the "I Didn't Understand" Form, the "I Was Deceived" Form, the List of Sins And Excuses, and a bunch of others. Fill them out and get them back to me. And don't forget to sign them all at the bottom—in blood, preferably.

CHRIS

[Eyeing the huge stage of papers on the clipboard.]
ALL of it?

[Meanwhile, OG-DUG sneaks over to the wall or pylon and seems to be drawing a picture on it, warily glancing over his shoulder at the CLERK.]

CLERK
Don't worry. You've got PLENTY of time. Take this number and go have a seat over there.
[Motions to row of seats.]

CHRIS
[Takes a number she hands him and is immediately horrified by the length of it.]
55,678,923,752!? You've got to be kidding! Well... what number are you on now?

CLERK
Two.

CHRIS
TWO!!!???

CLERK
Yep. Two.

CHRIS
Well... Who's Number Two?

CLERK
He's right over—
[Suddenly notices OG-DUG drawing on walls and shouts at him.]
Hey! OX-DUNG! You better not be drawing on the walls again!

OG-DUG
[Stops drawing and pounds his chest.]
Me Og-Dug! No Ox-Dung! Og-Dug!

CLERK
Whatever. Don't MAKE me come over there!

[OG-DUG shrugs, but drops to the floor, dumps the pile of sticks on the floor and rubs two of them together to try to start a fire.]

CLERK

[Mutters.]
Crazy cavemen!
[The calls back to him.]
Hey! Don't start a fire in here either!
[Muttering again.]
There'll be PLENTY of that where you're going.

[OG-DUG just turns his back to her and keeps working on his fire, rubbing the sticks together and blowing on it. (Careful to not REALLY start a fire!) Sometimes he might take a break and scratch or pick at his toes and eat things he finds on his body.]

CLERK

[Back to Chris.]
Well, go have a seat. You have a long wait in front of you.

CHRIS

[Finds a seat next to a woman in a suit who is reading a magazine.]
Hi, I'm Chris.

MARGARET

[Puts down her magazine.]
Margaret.
[They shake hands.]
Nice to meet you.

CHRIS

How long have you been here?

MARGARET

Oh, let me see... It's almost impossible to keep track of time in this place, but I'd guess about 50 years or so.

CHRIS

Wow!

MARGARET

Well, that's not so long as some. Like King Saul, over there.
[Motions toward KING SAUL, who waves.]

CHRIS

King Saul? From the Bible?

MARGARET

That's the theory. I, for one, don't believe everything I hear.

CHRIS

Like what?

MARGARET

Like that the Bible is true, for one. I mean, come on! Walking on water? The walls of a building falling down just because people are marching around it blowing on horns? I don't think so!

CHRIS

[No so sure as before.]
I know what you mean.... So, what's your story?

MARGERET

Well, I was taking a flight to a business conference and was just about to take a sip of my martini, and then somehow I ended up here. The rest is a little fuzzy.

CHRIS

So, what's your complaint?

MARGARET

Well, see, I'm an atheist. I don't believe in God at all, so I don't see why I have to go through this process just to rest in peace.

CHRIS

You don't believe in God? Even now? Don't you think being here would be something of a confirmation?

MARGARET
[Irritated.]
Well, do you see Him here anywhere, Mr. Smart Aleck?

CHRIS
No.

MARGARET
Alright, then!
[Goes back to reading her magazine.]

CHRIS
But obviously, if we're here, there's a lot more going on than we may have realized before.

[MARGARET is bent on ignoring him now, and just turns her back to him and keeps reading her magazine.]

CHRIS
I've got to get some more answers!
[Gets up to go back to the desk, when the phone rings and he has to wait.]

SOUND OF RINGING PHONE

CLERK
[Answers phone.]
Yeah.... Oh, hi, Frank.... No, your complaint hasn't been forwarded yet.... No.... No.... Look, Frank, you've really got to stop calling every century. You're not helping this process go any faster with your constant badgering! ...I understand, but please try to wait at least another millennia before calling again, alright? Bye.
[Hangs up and looks up at CHRIS.]
You, again?

CHRIS
Yes. I was just wondering what's really going on here.

CLERK

I thought I explained all of that already. You fill out the forms, you wait on the chairs, you leave me alone—simple!

CHRIS

No, that's not what I'm talking about. What's really going on? Behind the scenes?

CLERK

When we get your papers and your number is called, eventually, maybe, your case will be reviewed and you MIGHT get a chance to get out of here and get into Heaven somehow. We're working on it.
   [Goes back to filing her nails.]

CHRIS

   [Skeptically.]
Yeah... I can see that. But didn't you say you were on Number 2? So, it's possible that some people actually get through. Who was Number 1?

CLERK

Well... that's a bit of a story, see, Number 1 wasn't really Number 1. He got pushed to the front of the line on a technicality.

CHRIS

   [Excited.]
Well, what was the technicality?

CLERK

He was sinless.

CHRIS

What? How can that be?

CLERK

Don't ask me. Never saw it before nor since. Just this one Guy—name was Jesus—He said He'd never sinned. At first I didn't believe Him, but, sure enough, His chart was clean as whistle. Went straight on to Heaven, and I haven't seen Him since.

CHRIS
[Amazed and talking to himself.]
Jesus! You've got to be kidding me! And He didn't take anyone with Him?

CLERK
[Suddenly uncomfortable.]
Uh... I wouldn't know anything about that.

CHRIS
Well, then who would?

CLERK
[Trying to avoid eye-contact.]
You'll have to take that up with someone else. Go back to your seat now, please.
[Tries to wave him away.]

CHRIS
[Loud and angry.]
Look, I'm not going anywhere until I get some answers! What are you trying to hide?

CLERK
[Glances around nervously.]
Keep your voice down! ...Alright, I'll tell you! Just, don't spread this around, it could get me fired! And I mean LITERALLY FIRED!

CHRIS
[Lowers his voice.]
Alright.

CLERK
[Still very nervous.]
There HAS been a problem with disappearances. People come in here with these incredibly long lists of sins and once in a while—just when I'm about to have them take a number—this bright, blinding light shines in here from up above! At first I can't see anything, but when the light fades the first thing I notice is that the lists have been wiped completely clean and the client is gone. Vanished! But,

PLEASE, don't go spreading this around. If the boss found out, he'd be SO mad!

CHRIS

So, who were these people? Did they say anything?

CLERK

Yeah... they said they shouldn't be in here—of course, that's what everyone says, right? But they say that they are Christians, that Jesus already died for their sins and that—by some weird technicality—they can get through on HIS perfection! Can you believe that? I know, it's crazy, right? But the next thing I know they've gone missing, and I have a DEVIL of a time trying to cover their trails... no pun intended.

CHRIS

[Distraught.]

Well, did they all say the same thing? Didn't anybody manage to get through by some other way? Some way of working off the debt? Some other religion? Anything?

CLERK

Nope. Sorry, kid. But we're still working on it... you never know. We might come up with something eventually. Just fill out those forms and—

CHRIS

[Desperate.]

What for? I'm NEVER going to get out of here!

CLERK

Well, that's not EXACTLY true. You can always opt out of this process and go directly to Hell.

CHRIS

What did you say to me?

CLERK

Sorry, but that's your only other option. I suggest you just go back and sit down and relax for a while. Eventually we might—

CHRIS

No way! This isn't right! It can't be right! I can't be here! I'm getting out of here!

[He runs off back the way he came and soon disappears behind the low wall at the back of the stage.]

CLERK

[Standing and calling after him.]

Wait! Where do you think you're going?

[But it's too late and she shakes her head and sighs.]

Now, what am I going to tell the boss?

LIGHTS DIM AND FOCUS ON STAGE LEFT BACKSTAGE EXIT

[People on stage filter out quietly. REBECCA is walking back toward where she left CHRIS. CHRIS stumbles out from behind stage left rubbing his head. REBECCA sees him and runs over.]

LIGHTS CENTER ON CHRIS & REBECCA

REBECCA

Chris! Oh, my goodness, are you alright?

CHRIS

I don't know. I think I slipped and hit my head.

REBECCA

[Examining his head.]

Yep, you sure did. You've got a knot the size of a golf-ball. We should get you to a doctor.

CHRIS

No. Wait. Actually, before we do anything else… could you please tell me about this Jesus?

REBECCA

Well… sure!

[EXIT LEFT CHRIS and REBECCA, motioning like they're talking.]

THE END

Prison or Pardon?

Setting:
A jail cell.

Scripture Reference:
The Parable of the Sower   Matthew 13:1-23

Props:
Chains
A door made of bars (spray-painted PVC pipe or cardboard)
Fake rats
A lantern/light
Jingly key ring

Time Duration:
8-10 minutes

Characters:
NARRATOR:

PRISONER ONE: Dressed in rags

PRISONER TWO: Dressed in rags.

PRISONER THREE: Dressed in rags.

PRISONER FOUR: Dressed in rags.

RESCUER: Dressed in a long-sleeved, white robe,
                         like we imagine Jesus. Red welts painted
                         on his wrists that are, at first, hidden
                         from audience but revealed later.

Script:

[Scene opens with four PRISONERS chained to a wall or to posts in a jail cell.]

NARRATOR

The dark, damp cell smelled of mold and human waste. Rats scurried from one shadowed corner to another with no one to hinder them, and the lice and fleas mingled liberally on the feverish flesh of their human hosts. The prisoners received one meal a day—stale or wiggling with vermin—which they could barely reach for the thick iron shackles on arms and legs which anchored them securely to the brick wall [change to "post" if necessary]. Life—if one could call it that—limped on hour after hour in this dark, putrid hell.

It had been a long time since any of them had seen a clear shaft of light, but as the thick prison doors swung open, their cell was suddenly bathed in clarity—a clarity that illuminated the horrors around them.

[RESCUER opens jail door and shines light on prisoners. PRISONERS cover eyes and try to escape the light.]

All four inmates immediately covered their eyes at the sight of their condition. The first prisoner screamed out in anger.

PRISONER ONE

Shut the door! Shut the door!

NARRATOR

He couldn't bear to see the roaches swarming his food dish or the brown smears on the wall next to his head. It was too much to bear and he desperately sought the relief of darkness.

But the light didn't go away. It lingered and, though it caused pain to some, it was a miracle in itself. How long had they existed without the light? How long had they wallowed in darkness? How long had it been since their skin had felt warmth? Slowly, the light grew brighter. It drew nearer and bit by bit they could see it was coming from a lantern carried by a man.

[RESCUER moves closer to the prisoners. PRISONERS peak out from time to time, still wary of the light, but curious.]

Was it the jailer—that despicable monster who from time to time dropped in to torture and accuse? No. It was someone they had never seen before. Someone from the outside. A stranger.

PRISONER TWO
[Frightened.]
Who's there?

RESCUER
I have come to set you free.
[Lifts key ring, making them jingle.]
I have the key. Lift up your shackles that I might unlock them.

PRISONER ONE
It's too much! Stay away! The light is too much!

RESCUER
But you no longer have to live in darkness. I offer you freedom.

PRISONER ONE
It can't be. This squalor is too great. I don't believe you can free us. You came only to taunt us and to show us how horrible we are! Get away!

NARRATOR
No matter how the Rescuer tried to reassure the first prisoner, he would not listen. He closed his eyes tightly and turned his face to the wall. Eventually, the Rescuer moved on to the second man.

RESCUER
Let me free you from your chains.

PRISONER TWO

It sounds good… and I've heard that you have rescued others… but how do I know you're not here to trick me? How do I know you won't take me to a worse place than this?

RESCUER

Because I am the Rescuer. I hold the keys in my hand, and all I ask is that you allow me to unlock your chains. Then you may follow me and see freedom for yourself.

PRISONER TWO

[Extends his arms for a moment, but then withdraws them quickly before his shackles can be loosed.]
No. I'm sorry. It's simply too difficult to trust you. I think I would rather stay here—in a place I know rather than go with you.

RESCUER

Please. I promise I'll be with you every step of the way. Step into the light of freedom with me.

PRISONER TWO

No. I admit it's tempting, but the light can be a hard place to be—always seeing the ugliness that surrounds you, always aware of the filth that is life. It's too difficult a path for me. Thanks, but no thanks.

RESCUER

[Moves to the next prisoner.]
Accept the freedom I offer you. Please. I came a long way to set you free and have paid a great price. Don't stay in these miserable conditions any longer.

PRISONER THREE

[Extends arms eagerly.]
Yes! Set me free! You have no idea how much these shackles weigh

and how my skin has chaffed and broken beneath them! I want to be able to move about in freedom!

[RESCUER quickly unlocks the shackles and drops them to the floor. PRISONER THREE smiles broadly, stretches.]

RESCUER

Let me lead you out of this place. We have much to see and do.

PRISONER THREE

[Stops smiling and stares at RESCUER.]
Leave? To go where?

RESCUER

I will take you to my home where you will have a comfortable place to sleep, good food to eat, and friends who love you. You will work for me by helping to free others like yourself.

PRISONER THREE

But I can't leave the only home I've ever known. I know this place isn't much, but it's comfortable to me. And these people,
[Gestures to the other prisoners.]
well, they've become my friends. I can't leave them. No. I'm thankful to you for letting me out of my shackles, but I have no desire to leave this cell. I'm satisfied with what I have.

NARRATOR

Again, though he begged the third prisoner to reconsider, the Rescuer was flatly refused. Only one prisoner remained in the cell who had not yet received the Rescuer's invitation. He was smaller than the others, and his clothes even more ragged and foul smelling. When the light came near, he crouched a bit lower, but his eyes followed the stranger with deep interest.

RESCUER

I offer you freedom from the things that keep you captive. Extend your arms that I might release your chains.

PRISONER FOUR

But, Master… of all the criminals in this place, I am the worst. Why would you want to free someone like me? I deserve to be here.

RESCUER

Because your debt has already been paid. I have already taken your place.

[Extends wrists.]

NARRATOR

To the prisoner's surprise, the Rescuer extended his own arms, and the light revealed deep welts on his wrists that could only have been caused by thick, iron shackles like the ones the prisoners wore.

RESCUER

My father—the king of this land—has freed me, and now I am here to free you. If you come with me, your sins will be fully pardoned and my father will adopt you as a son. Together we will inherit a wonderful kingdom.

[PRISONER FOUR joyfully extends arms. As narrator reads, RESCUER unlocks the shackles and leads PRISONER FOUR from the cell, taking the light with him. EXIT PRISONER FOUR and RESCUER.]

NARRATOR

With tears of joy on his cheeks and relief in his eyes, the last prisoner extended his arms to the prince and allowed his shackles to be removed. Then, taking the hand of his Savior, he was led from the darkness of the prison cell into the light of a new life.

[EXIT PRISONERS ONE, TWO, and THREE and NARRATOR.]

THE END

What Am I Doing Wrong?
Part I

Setting:
In church

Time Duration:
1-2 minutes

Characters:
Change name of character depending on gender of the performers.

MARK or BETH: A Christian who feels it is his/her duty to save people.

BEN or LIZZIE: A non-Christian

Script:

[ENTER BEN stage right and MARK stage left.]

MARK
Hi, aren't you Ben?

BEN
Why, yes, and you are?

MARK
Name's Mark. Nice to see you again. I noticed you at church on Sunday.

BEN
Oh, right. I was visiting my family and they insisted I go. Plus, it was a potluck.

MARK
Oh, so you don't normally go to church?

BEN

No.

MARK

So, are you a Christian?

BEN

No. Never felt the need.

MARK

Oh, this is great!

BEN

[Stunned]
Wait... what? So, I guess you're not a Christian either.

MARK

Oh, I'm a Christian alright. It's just that our pastor keeps harping on us to get out and witness, but I never have the time due to my many, very spiritual Christian functions. So, I don't actually *know* any non-Christians to witness *to*—until now! And, to think I met you at church! Who'd'a thought one would show up there! It's kind of like a weird, cosmic mistake. Ha, ha, ha!

BEN

Yep. I know what you mean. I know *I'll* never make it again.
[Walks away. EXIT BEN.]

MARK

Hey, where are you going? I haven't even witnessed to you yet! Come back!
[Follows him off. EXIT MARK.]

TO BE CONTINUED...

What Am I Doing Wrong?
Part II

Setting: A coffee shop.

Props:
Small table
Two chairs
A newspaper
A coffee mug

Time Duration:
1-3 minutes

Characters:
Change name of character depending on gender of the performers.

MARK or BETH: A Christian who feels it is his/her duty to save people.

BEN or LIZZIE: A non-Christian

Script:

[BEN on stage sitting at a table, sipping a coffee and reading a newspaper.]

MARK
Oh, hi Ben! I'm so glad to see you!

BEN
Oh... hi, Mark. So I see you finally made it out of church to a coffee shop.

MARK
Oh, well, it's okay. It's Christian-owned. So, Ben, I've been meaning to talk to you—that is, if I ever saw you again. And here you are— what luck! Ha, ha, 'course I don't really believe in luck—good or bad.

BEN

Yeah, I know what you mean. I never believed in bad luck myself...
until now.

MARK

[Talks really fast.]

Speaking of beliefs, I wanted to share mine with you. Basically, God
made everything, including you and me. We were perfect, but then
we sinned. So, God sent Jesus to die on the cross for our sins so we
could be with Him in Heaven one day.

BEN

[Blank stare.]

MARK

So?

BEN

So... what?

MARK

So, what do you think?

BEN

About what?

MARK

About what I just said!? Don't you want to become a Christian?

BEN

Why would I want to do that?

MARK

Well, so you can go to Heaven one day, of course! Don't you want to
go to Heaven?

BEN

Sounds great, but....

MARK

Wonderful!
[Aside]
My pastor's going to be so stoked!!!
[To BEN]
So, just say this little prayer after me and you're in!: Dear Jesus, I know I'm a sinner....

BEN

[Blank stare]

MARK

[Louder and slower]
Dear Jesus, I know I'm a sinner....

BEN

Look, I don't think any of this is for me. I gotta run.
[Gets up and leaves. EXIT BEN.]

MARK

Wait! Come back! Hey, don't you know there's a Hell, too! …. Ah, man! Not again! What am I doing wrong?

[EXIT MARK.]

THE END

❧ SECTION FOUR ❧

Special Events

AND WE'RE BACK!

Usage/Purpose:

Use to announce a Back to School Party, the start-up of AWANA, a back-pack filling charity event for underprivileged school children, or to mark the transition between Sunday school classes as the kids graduate to higher grades.

Props:

2 Backpacks

Bag of School Supplies   (Packages of pencils, paper, rulers, glue sticks, erasers, pencil sharpeners, folders, notebooks, a box of Kleenex, etc.) Include a folder with a really girly front—sparkles, kittens, butterflies, etc.

Sheet of Paper with Typing on it.

Sound Effect:

Doorbell or Loud Knocking

Time Duration:

2-3 minutes

Characters:

MOM: Woman carrying a large back of school supplies and a sheet of paper

EDDIE: A little boy of about 10 or 12. Carries an empty backpack.

ANNIKA: A little girl of about 8 or 10. Carries an empty backpack.

CHRISSY: Homeschooled neighbor kid—aged 8-12. (Could

change to "CHRIS." Gender doesn't matter.)

Script:

[ENTER MOM with EDDIE and ANNIKA following.]

MOM

Alright, kids! Come on over here and we'll sort through this list your school sent me.

[Indicates sheet of paper. Then deposits bag of supplies on the floor CENTER STAGE. (Could also use a table.) Starts to pull things out of the bag, starting with girly folder.]

EDDIE

Wow! That's a lot of stuff! Do we really need all that?

MOM

Most of it—apparently—but I bought extra so we can donate what we don't use to kids whose parents can't afford to purchase everything on that list.

ANNIKA

I think that's a great idea!

EDDIE

Me, too!

[Picks up girly folder so audience can see it and makes a face.]
Ew! I think we should definitely donate this one!

ANNIKA

Hey! I like that one!

[Takes it from EDDIE, who gladly hands it over. Looks lovingly at the image on the folder.]
But... I guess some other girl might like it, too.... We can donate it, if you want to, Mom.

[Puts folder back on pile.]

MOM

Oh, I'm so proud of you, Annika! You are growing up into such a fine young lady!
[Looks at EDDIE.]
You, too, Eddie.

EDDIE

[Incensed.]
I'm growing up into a *fine young lady?*

MOM

[Laughing.]
No! No! I meant—

SOUND OF DOORBELL OR LOUD KNOCKING

ANNIKA

I'll get it!
[Runs to door. ENTER CHRISSY.]
Oh, hi, Chrissy! Come on in!

CHRISSY

[Joining them.]
Hi!

MOM

Hi, Chrissy! How's your mom doing these days? I haven't seen her out in her garden recently.

CHRISSY

Oh, she's been real busy with our homeschool lessons.

MOM

Oh, well, we're getting ready for school, too.

EDDIE

Yeah! School starts up again in two weeks [change as necessary] and we're just getting our school supplies sorted out.

ANNIKA

[A little sad.]
Yeah. Pretty soon our summer vacation will be over.

CHRISSY

[Immediately upset. Hands raised. Looking at EDDIE and ANNIKA. Firmly, loudly, and slowly.]
Whoa, whoa, whoa! Wait just one second! *You* mean to tell me that you get a *SUMMER VACATION?*

[MOM, EDDIE, and ANNIKA just look at each other with a surprised and a little guilty expression on their faces, like they were caught in the act. Pause on that for a moment. Then EXIT ALL.]

THE END

Batter Up!

Usage/Purpose:
Use to announce an upcoming baby dedication ceremony.

Props/Preparations:
8-10 baby dolls, tied to a long rope in a line. This line of babies is suspended across the stage, babies facing outwards.
Small Bible.

Time Duration:
2-3 minutes

Characters:
PASTOR: Pastor

STELLA: Church pianist.

Script:

[Scene opens with PASTOR standing CENTER STAGE behind the row of babies. He is near the first one and is holding a small Bible, muttering to himself. ENTER STELLA.]

STELLA
Pastor? You over here? I was just coming to practice that song for the baby dedication next Sunday and—
[Stops short, seeing line of baby dolls.]
Oh, my goodness! What in the world are you doing?

PASTOR
Oh, hi, Stella. I'm just practicing up for the baby dedication. I haven't done one of these in a while and I'm a little nervous.

STELLA

Good grief! Is it going to be a baby dedication or are you planning on hanging them all out to dry?

PASTOR

Relax! I got the idea from my son's baseball practice yesterday. They stuck all the balls in that machine, and it just shot out one after another at the batter. Like an assembly line of practice. So, I adapted the idea and wha-lah! An assembly line of babies to dedicate!

[Looks proudly at his invention.]

STELLA

Well, I guess I should be glad you're not shooting babies all over the sanctuary....

PASTOR

[Excited.]

Look, this is how it works. I just start here at the first baby, run through my blessing and prayer and comments to the parents, and then move on to the next one. By my third time through the line, I won't even have to look at the Bible!

STELLA

Wow... OK. That's not weird.

PASTOR

I can already recite the entire blessing in under four seconds! Wanna hear it?

STELLA

Oh, I'm sure I'll hear it on Sunday.

[Laughs.]

Look, I'm sure you'll do fine at the dedication. And there's nothing wrong with a little practice but this... well, this is... is.... Um.... Why don't we just take this down before any of the parents see it, okay?

PASTOR

Oh, alright! I guess I got in enough practice for one day.

[PASTOR and STELLA start to untie the ends of the rope.]

But, hey. Don't untie those babies yet. I want to take this home and show my wife! She's got an awards banquet coming up!

STELLA

Oh, dear!

[EXIT ALL.]

THE END

Come With Me

Purpose/Usage:
To announce an upcoming youth retreat or special event. Could be adapted to use as an evangelistic skit for inviting people to church or regular church events.

Setting:
A high-school lunch room or yard where kids are sitting around eating lunch.

Props:
Lunch bags
Paper sacks
Lunch trays with fake food on them
Backpacks
Books/Papers

Time Duration:
Approximately 2-3 minutes

Characters:
JENNY: A Christian teen

ALLIE: A non-Christian friend from school.

EXTRAS: (Optional) Other kids who sit No lines.

Script:

[ENTER ALLIE and EXTRAS. ALLIE sits alone. EXTRAS sit in small groups around the stage, pretending to eat lunch in small groups while talking together or texting or studying. EXTRAS just pretend to do this things, and make no noise.]

[ENTER JENNY. She walks through with her lunch bag, spots ALLIE, and sits down with her.]

JENNY

Oh, hey, Allie!

ALLIE

[Looking up]
Oh, hi, Jenny. How are you doing?

JENNY

Not bad. World history is about to sink me, though. I think Mr. Franklin thinks it's a college class, not a high school class. He wants us to come up with twenty sources for our research paper! Twenty!

ALLIE

Yuck! I'm glad I got Miss Miller. She's the best.

JENNY

Yeah, I heard she gives out full-sized snicker bars for A's and B's on her exams. I'm so jealous!

ALLIE

[Laughs and pats stomach.]
Yep! I'll be a few sizes larger by the end of the year.

JENNY

[Laughs, too. Then continues.]
Hey, I know you're going to visit your grandma this weekend, but what are you going to do the weekend after that?

ALLIE

Don't know. But you better not ask me to come help you with your research paper. Sorry, sister, you're on your own.
[Snickers.]

JENNY

[Laughing.]
No, no! Don't worry. I've got my mom for that. Actually, I wanted invite you to go on a youth retreat with me.

ALLIE

[Grows serious, hesitant.]
Oh, is this one of those church youth group things you're always inviting me to?

JENNY

Yes. Yes, it is. But it's to [ENTER NAME OF PLACE] and we're going to have SO much fun! The kids are really nice and the leaders are great. You'll have a blast, I promise! And I'll be there with you the whole time!

ALLIE

I don't know…

JENNY

[Sing-song voice, trying to tempt her.]
There'll be food… maybe even Snickers ….

ALLIE

[Smirks, but still serious.]
But, you know how I feel about organized religion.

JENNY

[Confident.]
Then you should definitely come! We're not organized at all.

ALLIE

[Laughing.]
OK, OK… I guess I can ask my dad, at least.

JENNY

Awesome! I'll text you all the details, and I'll call you later so we can decide what to wear!

ALLIE

[Smiling, more relaxed.]
OK, sounds good. …Oh, and thanks, Jenny.

[EXIT ALL.]

THE END

The Gift That Keeps On Giving

(A version of this skit was originally developed and performed by Rev. David and Carol Brown. Adapted and used here by permission.)

Purpose/Usage:
To announce and promote Operation Christmas Child, a ministry of The Samaritan's Purse.

Props:
A shoebox with a hole in the bottom.
Lid to the shoebox.
A table or frame with a hole in the top. You can also use a larger box with a hole in the bottom turned upside down.
A tablecloth to completely cover the table/frame/larger box. Tablecloth also has a hole in the middle.
A large box.
A large bag filled with the following:
>A big teddy bear.
>A dozen or so toothbrushes.
>A dozen or so new containers of toothpaste.
>Several packages of soap, double-bagged.
>Several packages of pencils, erasers, and pencil sharpeners.
>Several large spiral notebooks.
>A large bag of hard candy.
>Several new washcloths and pairs of socks.
>Miscellaneous toys, hairbands, and novelties.

Preparations:
Before service starts, place table/frame/larger box on stage. Place large box beneath the table so that the opening is up. Place tablecloth on top of table so that it completely covers both the table and the box beneath and so that the holes all line up. The idea is to make it so that it looks like a regular, covered table, but it is secretly hollow. A shoebox must be able to sit on top, with the hole in its bottom lining up with the hole in the top of the table, so that anything placed in the shoebox will mysteriously disappear (falling into the box beneath).

Time Duration:
Approximately 7-10 minutes

Characters:
(Feel free to use actors' real names. Gender doesn't matter.)
MAVIS
RODNEY

Script:

[ENTER MAVIS and RODNEY. RODNEY is carrying a large bag filled with Operation Christmas Child donations. MAVIS is carrying an empty shoebox (that has a false bottom). MAVIS places the box on the table, and they both turn to the audience.]

MAVIS

Hello everyone! Rodney and I are so excited to be here this morning because today we're going to talk about a wonderful event that our church gets to participate in this fall—Operation Christmas Child! On [DATE]_____ we are going to collect shoeboxes you have filled and then donate them to children all over the world! Now, of course, the first thing you need to learn is how to fill your boxes— what to put in them and what NOT to put in them. So, that's why Rodney and I are here today!

[Indicates shoebox.]
Now, please use a standard size shoe-box—not a giant one for boots or a tiny one for baby shoes. Make sure your shoebox is about this size. If you use a shoebox from home, you can wrap it in pretty Christmas paper. Just be sure to wrap the bottom and the lid separately, so that the boxes can be opened. Before they can be shipped, they first have to be inspected and a small booklet with the salvation message in the child's language will be added to each one. You can also use a box we will provide to you OR you can purchase a plastic shoe-boxed sized Rubbermaid container and fill that.

The next thing you need to know is what NOT to buy. Please DO NOT put anything liquid in your shoebox. No shampoos or perfumes. Don't put in anything that will easily break. Don't put used items in your box. New gifts only, please. Please don't put in violent toys, like toy soldiers or toy guns as many of these gifts are going to war-ravaged areas. Also, these boxes may be sitting in a hot plane for several hours, so DON'T put anything that will melt, like chocolate or tootsie rolls. Rodney here will be confiscating all the chocolate.

[RODNEY smiles, nods, and rubs belly.]

MAVIS

OK! So, now let's talk about what you SHOULD put in your shoebox. We'd like each child to receive at least one nice gift. You get to choose whether to buy for a boy or girl aged 2 to 4, a boy or girl aged 5 to 9, or a boy or girl, aged 10 to 14. A small child might like a stuffed animal, while an older child might prefer jewelry or a deflated soccer ball. You decide.

[RODNEY pulls out oversized teddy bear. MAVIS notices and is shocked.]

MAVIS

Oh, no! Rodney, I'm sorry, but there's no way that teddy bear is going to fit in that small box! We're going to have to—

[RODNEY ignores MAVIS and shoves the bear into the box, making sure the whole thing goes through the hole and falls into the large, hidden box beneath.]

MAVIS

Well, my goodness! I guess I was wrong! [Looks at RODNEY, looks in box, then looks back to RODNEY in surprise.] OK, well, you might also want to give your child some personal hygiene items, like soap, a new toothbrush, and a box of toothpaste.

[RODNEY pulls out these items as she's speaking. He begins to drop copious amounts of each item into the box as she speaks, making sure the audience can see the items first. MAVIS, for now, is ignoring him.]

MAVIS

You only need to give each child one of each item. Also, consider adding some school supplies to your Christmas box. In our country pencils are easy to come by, but in some places of the world, an entire classroom full of children may have to share a single one.

[RODNEY pulls out the school supplies and drops them in as she lists them off.]

MAVIS
[Speaking slowly.]
So, pencils and pencil sharpeners are wonderful things to add. So are erasers and small notebooks, if you can get them to fit.

[RODNEY is pushing large notebooks into the box. MAVIS finally sees what he's doing.]

MAVIS
Rodney! Good grief! What are you doing?

RODNEY
I'm filling my shoebox, just like you told me.

MAVIS
Oh, really? JUST like I told you?

[RODNEY nods.]

MAVIS
[Sighs.] Look, just try not to go overboard, okay? We need to make sure everything fits.

[RODNEY nods again.]

MAVIS
Alright, where was I? Oh! If you add soap, be sure to double-bag it and put it on the opposite side of the box from the candy. We don't want our candy tasting like soap! Oh, candy! I forgot to tell you to add candy. Hard candy only, of course! Remember, don't add anything that will melt! The candy also has to be double-bagged.

[RODNEY retrieves the large bag of hard candy, opens it and just dumps the whole thing into the box, making sure it all disappears inside.]

MAVIS

[Notices RODNEY.]

Merciful heavens, Rodney! You're not very good at following directions, are you?

[RODNEY just grins sheepishly and tries to toss the empty candy bag away so she won't see.]

MAVIS

[To RODNEY.]

Now, please try to behave! It's very important that these folks learn the directions. Hopefully, they can follow them better than you can! [Turns to audience.] OK, one final thing. If there is any space left in your box, go ahead and fill it with other things these kids might need or want. A pair of clean socks or maybe a new washcloth.

[RODNEY adds several of each item as she talks.]

MAVIS

Small toys, hair ribbons, and gifts are great! Remember, this may be the only Christmas gift these kids ever get, so make it a great one! Lastly, each box requires an additional [AMOUNT] _____ dollars to cover the shipping.

[Add whether they need to pay this or if the church is going to take up a special offering to cover the shipping costs. Also, you can add how many boxes your church filled last year and/or what your goal amount is for this year.]

Feel free to include a personal photo and a message or card to the child who receives your gift.

[MAVIS turns to RODNEY.]

Rodney, is there anything else they need to know?

RODNEY

Just one more thing. Be sure to pray for the children who receive these gifts. Ask God to bless them and their families and bring them to a saving knowledge of Jesus Christ! And, remember, we can't supply all of their needs, but He can! He is the one who multiplied five fish and two loaves of bread to feed 5,000 people, and He can multiply your gift, too! Your gift will be a real blessing, but Jesus is the gift that keeps on giving! So ask Him to go along with your gift!

[RODNEY puts the lid on the shoebox. EXIT MAVIS and RODNEY, leaving everything behind on the stage to be cleaned up later.]

THE END

Koinenea Gals, Won't You Come Out Tonight?

Suggested Usage:
This skit is perfect for a women's retreat or to accompany a church announcement about a women's event.

Props:
Bible for ELVIRA
Hillbilly clothing

Time Duration:
Approximately 6-8 minutes.

Characters:
All characters are dressed in loud, hillbilly dresses or overalls. Hair in pigtails, braids, curlers, etc... Be creative!

BETTY

LORETTA

MARY-SUE

LOU-ELLEN

ELVIRA   Has a Bible hidden somewhere on her person.

BONNY

Script:

> [Off stage the sound of merry singing can be heard and it grows louder. The song is "Buffalo Gals, Won't You Come Out Tonight?" except substituting the word "Koinenea" for "Buffalo." Enter ALL except BETTY. They are arm in arm, kicking up their heels and singing gaily. After a while their song dies out and they look around as if someone is missing.]

LOU-ELLEN
Betty! Betty, where'd you git off to, girl? Betty!!!

BONNY

Well, where'd she go?

LOU-ELLEN

Now, Betty, I *know* yer back there, now git yerself on out 'cheer right now!

BETTY

[From off stage.]
I'm not comin' out, so you kin jus' forgit it!

MARY-SUE

What seems to be the trouble, Betty?

BETTY

[Still from off stage.]
I ain't sayin', Mary-Sue!

ELVIRA

Look, woman, we came here as at the Koinenea Gals. Koinenea means fellowship. Now is you is, or is you ain't gonna git on out cheer and start in to fellowshippin' with us?

BONNY

Elvira, somehow I don't think that's gonna make her want to come out.

LORETTA

OK! Hold on there, ladies. Loretta'll take care of this!

[LORETTA leaves and comes back dragging a reluctant BETTY with her onto the stage.]

BETTY

Alright, alright! I'm here already! Are ya happy now?

LOU-ELLEN

What's the matter with you, girl? Don'cha wanna be with yer friends this weekend?

BETTY

Not dressed like this! I look like a sumo wrestler in drag! I cain't believe ya'll made me wear this getup!

MARY-SUE

You know, Betty, it don't matter what you look like on the outside—just what you look like on the inside.

LORETTA

I think it looks mighty nice... almost as nice as mine...
   [Does some smoothing and primping.]

BONNY

Betty, are your clothes the real reason you didn't want to come with us this weekend?

BETTY

Well... not totally, no—but I wasn't exageratin' about how I look! I look like a 'coon thet jus' got chased by a weed-whacker, an thet's the truth!

LOU-ELLEN

So, what's the problem then? We're all your friends here.

ELVIRA

Of course we are... Now spit it out so we kin' git on to the fun stuff!

BETTY

Well, it's jus' thet it feels like everybody else here is so... so much more... oh, how do I say... so much more spiritual than I am.

BONNY

What? What do you mean?

MARY-SUE

Oh, don't be silly! What's that supposed to mean, anyway?

ELVIRA

Well, slap my knee and make me eat possum, ladies. I mean, she may have a point. After all, some of us *are* pretty spiritual.

[She pulls a Bible out of her skirt or somewhere.]
It could be intimidatin'.

[BETTY looks even more depressed.]

LORETTA

Now, Betty, don't you pay her no never'mind! Don' think thet jus' because you made mistakes in your life thet you cain't be a part of this family!

BONNY

Thet's right, sweetheart!

LOU-ELLEN

Let's read her thet verse—you know, the one about the Koinenea girls. I believe it's Colossians 3:12-17.

ELVIRA

Well, butter my behind an' call me a biscuit. I got me a Bible right 'cheer. I'll look it up.
[She fumbles around for a while. The others start to get impatient with her.]
Hmmm. Where's Colossians again?… Oh, there it is! Alright, I got it!
[She reads the verse in a thick southern accent with lots of gestures.] "Therefore, as God's chosen people, holy and dearly loved, clothe yourselves with compassion, kindness, humility, gentleness, and patience. Bear with each other and forgive whatever grievances you may have against one another. Forgive as the Lord forgave you. And over all these virtues put on love, which binds them all together in perfect unity. Let the peace of Christ rule in your hearts, since as members of one body you were called to peace. And be thankful. Let the word of Christ dwell in you richly as you teach and admonish one another with all wisdom, and as you sing psalms, hymns and spiritual songs with gratitude in your hearts to God. And whatever you do, whether in word or deed, do it all in the name of the Lord Jesus, giving thanks to God the Father through him."

BETTY

That sure is a nice passage, ain't it?

MARY-SUE

It's more than that! It shows us how we're supposed to treat each other—not jus' on special weekends, but all the time! Jesus is supposed to shine through us all the time!

LOU-ELLEN

An' so if we're not bein' thet way, it's OUR problem—certainly not yours!

BONNY

An' thet place where it says to forgive one another—if someone here don't treat you right, you'll jus' have to forgive *us*... because maybe, jus' maybe we're not as spiritual as you think we are.

LORETTA

[Looking at Elvira who is scratching herself.]
An' we're certainly not as spiritual as *we* think we are.

MARY-SUE

So, we jus' need to come together an' help each other out—jus' like a real, close-like family!

BETTY

Well, I guess I could do thet.

LOU-ELLEN

Come on, ladies. How does thet song go agin?

[They break into song again and wrap their arms around each other and walk off stage again.]

ALL

[Singing.]
Koinenea Gals, won't you come out tonight? Come out tonight? Come out tonight? Koinenea Gals, won't you come out tonight? And dance by the light of the moon!....

[EXIT ALL.]

THE END

A Little Help, Please?

Purpose/Usage:
Use this skit to show appreciation for your pastor(s) and family(ies) on Pastor Appreciation Sunday (2nd Sunday of October) or to announce an event where the pastor(s) and family(ies) will be honored—perhaps when they retire or move.

Scene: Pastor's office. There is a table and chair with various papers and a pencil on the table. There is a sign on it that says "PASTOR".

Sound Effects:
There needs to be a way for them to knock loudly or use a digital sound effect.

Time Duration:
5 minutes

Characters:
PASTOR

SANDRA   Carries a very long, rolled up list.

FRED

BLAINE

JOYCE

Script:

[Enter PASTOR. He sits down at the table and begins to work. Enter SANDRA. She knocks but goes right in.]

SANDRA
Oh, good! I caught you!

PASTOR
[Pleasantly.]

Oh, good morning, Sandra. How can I help you?

SANDRA
Well, I'm glad you asked. I'm here because I'd like to get marriage counseling.

PASTOR
Marriage counseling? But, Sandra, you're not married.

SANDRA
Well, not yet.

PASTOR
Oh! I understand! You must mean *pre-marital* counseling! I think congratulations are in order! Who's the lucky guy?
[Stands up and reaches out hand to shake hers, but she declines.]

SANDRA
No, Pastor, I'm not engaged yet.

PASTOR
[Confused. Sits back down.]
I don't understand.

SANDRA
You see, I want marriage counseling—counseling on how I might go about getting married. I need you to help me find Mr. Right.

PASTOR
[Baffled.]
You want me to get you a date?

SANDRA
Not just a date! I want you to find me someone with marriageable qualities. See, I even brought a list. I wrote down everything I want in a man.
[Pulls out list and unrolls it, letting it roll across the floor.]
He's got to have black hair, be dashingly handsome—but not better looking than me, of course, tall, and
[dreamily and with an English accent]

have eyes like the sea after a storm...

PASTOR

Sandra, I don't think you know what marriage counseling is all about, see—

[Enter Fred. His loud knock interrupts.]

FRED

Hey, there, Pastor! Can we talk?

PASTOR

Well, sure, Fred, but I'm talking with—

FRED

Oh, perfect!
[Ignoring SANDRA completely. She doesn't seem to mind too much. She's sizing him up.]
See, something happened to me yesterday and it's been bothering me ever since.

PASTOR

You do look rather distraught.

FRED

I am, Pastor! I surely am! You see, my faith is in danger!

PASTOR

What? That's terrible. Tell me about it.

FRED

Well, I was driving along looking for a parking space just before the football game last night. And there weren't any.

PASTOR

Sounds typical for a football game.

FRED

But I prayed, Pastor! I prayed so hard! I said, "Lord, if You're really real, please show me, Your humble servant, who's just trying to see the Bears [REPLACE WITH A LOCAL TEAM] kick the pants off somebody for ONCE, find a parking space." But, Pastor, He didn't do it! There just weren't any! I ended up having to walk six blocks! And the Bears lost! …Pastor, what does it mean?

PASTOR
Well, Fred, I…

[Before he can answer, another knock. ENTER BLAINE.]

BLAINE
Pastor?

PASTOR
Hello, Blaine.

BLAINE
You promised to help me install my carpet this afternoon, remember?

PASTOR
Oh, yes, that's right. I'll be there; I promise.

BLAINE
Oh, good! I'm glad you're still available, because I told my neighbor's second cousin's babysitter that you'd help her, too. She's a got a piano that needs to be moved from the first floor to the fifth floor. You don't mind, do you?

PASTOR
Well, I…

[Another knock. ENTER JOYCE.]

JOYCE
Oh, hey! It's a party!

PASTOR
Hi, Joyce.
[Giving up.]

Won't you join us?

JOYCE
Well, sure! In fact, I have something to ask you.

PASTOR
Sure you do.

JOYCE
Actually, this is quite serious. Last week I went out of town to visit my aunt, and we decided we should go to church together. But, Pastor, my sister goes to a Presbyterian
[REPLACE WITH A DIFFERENT DENOMINATION FROM YOUR OWN]
church. Yes, I know! Anyway, that Sunday they had a potluck dinner, and well, my question is this: Is it okay for Baptists
[REPLACE WITH YOUR DENOMINATION]
to eat the food offered to Presbyterians
[REPLACE]?

SANDRA
Hey! There's nothing wrong with Presbyterians! My mom's a Presbyterian! Besides, I was here first. I think he should answer my question first.

FRED
Oh, hi Sandra. When did you get here?

SANDRA
Pastor,
[pretending to whisper and covering mouth with one hand]
he is *definitely not* Mr. Right!

BLAINE
Pastor, my carpet?

JOYCE
Pastor, the Presbyterians?

SANDRA

Pastor, my man?

FRED

Pastor, my parking space?

PASTOR

[Gets up to leave.]
You know what? I think all of you should pay a visit to Pastor Bob.
[REPLACE WITH NAME OF YOUR ASSISTANT PASTOR
OR AN ELDER.]
His office is right over there.
[Points in the opposite direction.]

[As they all turn to look, and Pastor ducks out the back. Exit Pastor.]

ALL

Hey, where did he go? Pastor?

FRED

[Quickly heading off.]
Hey, Pastor Bob!

[The rest follow him out, competing for first place at Pastor Bob's desk. EXIT ALL.]

THE END

What's Your Problem?
A Game Show

Purpose/Usage Suggestions:
This skit is designed as a bit of fun for use during a ladies' retreat or to use to accompany an announcement of an upcoming ladies' event. It could also be fun to vary the genders and use it during a Valentine's banquet or church potluck/picnic. Feel free to change descriptions of characters depending on the genders of your actors.

Setting:
This is a variation of the dating game. Arrange five chairs on stage with four close to one another in a line, facing the audience, and the fifth a little further off, but also facing the audience.

Team Leader Directions: It is best if this is run like a real game. So, no rehearsal is required, but some adlibbing is. The person playing the doctor must not know what the secret ailments of the contestants are. She must actually guess. Be sure, when you copy and give this script to your contestants, that you *omit the section below above "Script"* or you will spoil the surprise. In addition to the script, make a copy of the "Directions" sections, cut them out, and give one to each of your contestants. They should not see one another's problem previous to the game show. Remember to keep the show going and not to let it drag. You can try to prompt the contestants to answer the question, but not all of them will. If they don't, move on.

Characters
GAME SHOW HOST:	This role could be played by the team leader.
DR. IMA WELLCHICK	
CONTESTANT NUMBER ONE:	Carries sign & a basket with eggs in the bottom
CONTESTANT NUMBER TWO:	Carries sign & a bottle of water.

| CONTESTANT NUMBER THREE: | Carries sign & a roll of paper towels. |
| CONTESTANT NUMBER FOUR: | Carries sign. |

Props:
5 Chairs
Microphones, as needed
Basket with eggs in it for contestant number one. (Try to keep the eggs from being visible to either the doctor or the audience.)
Bottle of water for contestant number two.
Roll of paper towels for contestant number three.
Sign for Contestant Number One: Believes She Is Turning Into The Easter Bunny
Sign for Contestant Number Two: Too Much Botox
Sign for Contestant Number Three: Zero Bladder Control
Sign for Contestant Number Four: Wants to Marry Her Mailbox

Time Duration:
20-25 minutes

Directions for Contestant Number One:
Keep your sign hidden from everyone until it's your turn to answer a question. Then hold it up for the audience to see, *but not the doctor.* When you get up to the stage, you place your basket on the floor. You believe you are turning into the Easter Bunny. This process happens gradually. In three stages, coinciding with your turn to answer the question, you begin to develop bunny-like symptoms. Answer the first question with things like, "Springtime in a big, grassy yard." Engage in nose-twitching, the imaginary growth of long ears, a desire to scratch your arm (or ear, if you can reach) with your foot— all show up in the first round. In the second round, get down on all fours and begin to hop around. Pester the other guests by sniffing their legs, eventually make your way back to your chair. Answer the question with "dogs." In the third round, you are fully the Easter Bunny. Ignore the question if you want. Retrieve your basket and start hopping around (upright) and leaving eggs around the stage.

Directions for Contestant Number Two:

Keep your sign hidden from everyone until it's your turn to answer a question. Then hold it up for the audience to see, *but not the doctor.* Your lips are so swollen you can't talk right. Feel free to stuff your lips with cotton, if you want, but be sure to slur your words. Answer the first question with "The Bahamas, eating bananas and having a fish fry." Of course, you'll say it more like "Babamas, eebing bamamas and habing a bish by." Starting on the second question, take a drink from your water bottle and let it dribble all down your front. Then answer, "Bad doctors." On third question, take another drink and again make a mess with it. Feel free to "accidentally" get some on the contestants next to you. Answer, "I'll be a millionaire from the money from my lawsuit." Be sure to slur it! It doesn't matter if people understand you or not.

Directions for Contestant Number Three:

Keep your sign hidden from everyone until it's your turn to answer a question. Then hold it up for the audience to see, *but not the doctor.* Hold the roll of paper towels on your lap. As the game goes on, you get more and more agitated. You really have to pee, and it's getting worse all the time! Take some paper towels off the roll and place them across your chair. Then sit down again. Keep doing this throughout each question/answer session. Answer the first question with, "A girl's locker room—or, better yet, a big swimming pool!" Twitch on your chair, cross your legs, fidget. More paper towels. On the second question, answer, "Waterfalls." On the third question, add more paper towels. Then get up and do a little potty dance. Answer with, "I might have a dancing career." When the game is over, make fast tracks out of the room!

Directions for Contestant Number Four:

Keep your sign hidden from everyone until it's your turn to answer a question. Then hold it up for the audience to see, *but not the doctor.* On the first question, answer, "Probably standing out by the curb in my front yard—just staring at the one I love." Answer the second question with, "Being judged for who—or what—I choose to love. I mean, the laws are changing, right? And, even though my mother said to avoid relationships with red flags, what if it just has one? At least I'm involved with mail." Answer the third question saying, "Married, with a whole bunch of little letters and packages and postcards."

Script:

[The Doctor is on stage, sitting in the fifth chair. The host stands in the front of the stage.]

GAME SHOW HOST

Welcome everyone to this episode of "What's Your Problem?" the game show where one lucky contestant can win a full, expense-paid visit with our illustrious doctor, Dr. Ima Wellchick, expert in all things physiological, mental, and imaginary.

[Turns to Dr. IMA WELLCHICK.]

Doctor, won't you please stand up and bow for our audience?

DR. IMA WELLCHICK

[Stands up and bows. Gushes.]
Thank you all so much for having me here today! I'm so very honored to be here with you. You are a wonderful audience and—

GAME SHOW HOST

[Loudly interrupting.]
Alright, alright! Go back to your seat. We've got a lot to do today.

DR. IMA WELLCHICK

Well, I never!
[Flustered and annoyed, returns to her seat.]

GAME SHOW HOST

It's time for our contestants to come up on stage.

CONTESTANTS ONE, TWO, THREE, and FOUR

[Come up and take a seat in the appropriate order.]

GAME SHOW HOST

As you know, the point of this game is for the contestants to describe their ailments to our good doctor here without revealing what their problem really is. The doctor will ask three questions, which each contestant will have a chance to answer. Then the doctor must try to guess what each contestant's problem is. She gets two guesses per contestant. Whoever's problem she guesses correctly wins the doctor's visit! More than one winner is possible! Does everyone understand?

[Explain again if anyone is confused, then move on. Turn to DR. IMA WELLCHICK.]

Alright, Doctor, go ahead and ask your first question!

DR. IMA WELLCHICK

Alright, Contestants. My first question is this: What is your dream vacation?

[Listen and observe as each contestant answers. *Do not read what's on their signs as they hold them up!*]

GAME SHOW HOST

Okay.... Not sure how helpful that was. So, Dr., go ahead and ask your second question!

DR. IMA WELLCHICK

Very, well. My second question is this: What is your biggest fear?

[Listen and observe as each contestant answers.]

GAME SHOW HOST

Wow! Not sure where this is heading. But, Dr., go ahead and ask your third and final question!

DR. IMA WELLCHICK

My third question is this: Where do you see yourself five years from now?

[Listen and observe as each contestant answers.]

GAME SHOW HOST

Okay, Doctor! It's time for you to guess. What are their problems?

DR. IMA WELLCHICK

[Do your best to guess what each contestant's problem is.]

GAME SHOW HOST

[At the end of the game, reiterate who won the contest and the free doctor's visit. Wish them well, and thank the doctor for coming. Dismiss the contestants and the doctor. Then thank the audience for being a "lovely audience" and for watching this morning's episode of "What's Your Problem?"]

[EXIT ALL.]

THE END

✺ Section FIVE ✺

Holidays

Awkward Moments

Theme:
Valentine's Day. This could be used as a fun way to announce a church Valentine's Day banquet or single's outing.

Setting:
A nice restaurant with a single table set up for a romantic date night.

Props/Decorations:
A small table
Two chairs
A tablecloth
Two basic table settings (plate, cup, fork, napkin)
A flower in a small vase as a centerpiece (and/or something Valentine's Day themed)
Pitcher
2 menus
White hand towel
Sound Track: Various burping noises.
Piggy bank
Toenail clippers

Time Duration:
7-10 minutes

Characters:
WAITER	Could be a boy or a girl. Dressed in black slacks and white shirt like a waiter. Wears hand towel over one arm.
BOY ONE	Dressed nicely.
GIRL ONE	Dressed nicely.
BOY TWO	Dressed nicely.
GIRL TWO	Dressed nicely.
BOY THREE	Dressed nicely. Has a piggy bank, toenail clippers, and
GIRL THREE	Dressed nicely.

Script:

[ENTER WAITER, BOY ONE, and GIRL ONE. WAITER
seats BOY ONE and GIRL ONE, hands them the menus, and
pretends to fill their glasses with water. BOY ONE and GIRL
ONE settle in and put napkins on their laps. EXIT WAITER.]

BOY ONE
[Nervously.]
Wow, you actually came—I mean, it's so nice to finally get out... to
get you out... to get to go out with you, um... here... at this place...
restaurant.

GIRL ONE
Oh, right! Yes. This is nice. Thanks so much for inviting me! I was
really surprised when you asked me. I didn't think you knew who I
was.

BOY ONE
Oh! Everyone knows who you are! You're the captain of the
cheerleading team! That's why Jason dared me to do it.
[Slaps hand over mouth.]

GIRL ONE
[Angry.]
Wait one second! What? You were *dared* to ask me out on a date?

BOY ONE
[Talking fast.]
Well, it's just that I'm shy, and I couldn't... um... and then he was
like, 'why don't you?' and I was like, 'I don't know,' and he was like,
'I'll double-dog dare you,' and I was like, 'you're a jerk,' and he was
like—

GIRL ONE

[Interrupting.]

Wait, wait, wait! You weren't only *dared* to go out with me, but you think he's a jerk for getting you into this mess? Am I that horrible of a date? [Stands up, drops menu, and throws napkin back on table.] I'm out of here!

[EXIT GIRL ONE.]

BOY ONE

Wait! Please! Don't go!....

[Hand out toward her. Then, meekly.]

You're pretty....

[Finally, hangs head, sighs, and gets up.]

[EXIT BOY ONE. ENTER WAITER. He/She is confused that his/her customers have gone missing. Shrugs shoulders and fixes table again.]

[ENTER BOY TWO and GIRL TWO. WAITER seats BOY TWO and GIRL TWO, hands them the menus, and pretends to fill their glasses with water. BOY TWO and GIRL TWO settle in and put napkins on their laps. EXIT WAITER.]

BOY TWO

Man, I'm starving! It's been a whole hour since my last meal!

GIRL TWO

Wow... OK.

[Tries to smooth it over with a good-natured laugh.]

You sure do have quite an appetite!

BOY TWO

Where'd that waiter go?

[Looks at menu.]

I'm going to get the appetizer sampler platter, the double-decker hamburger with the bottomless fries, a plate of shrimp ka-bobs on the side, and the extra-large, triple berry smoothie!

GIRL TWO

Good grief!
[Chuckles. Then, sarcastically:]
What, no dessert?

BOY TWO

Oh, right! This apple pie alamode looks good. Hmmm… I wonder if I should get the slice or go ahead and get the whole pie….

GIRL TWO

That's going to be quite a bill.

BOY TWO

Oh, that reminds me. I'm going to have to ask you to float me on this one. I forgot my wallet at home.

GIRL TWO

What? Seriously?

BOY TWO

Yeah. I'll pay you back… eventually. I mean, what are friends for?

GIRL TWO

[Angrily, slamming her menu on the table.]
Friends? I thought this was a date!

BOY TWO

Wait…. What did I say?

GIRL TWO

[Stands up and throws napkin back on table.]

Oh, I don't know…. Why don't you go ask one of your *friends* to explain it to you?

[Stomps off.]

[EXIT GIRL TWO.]

BOY TWO

Hey! Where are you going?

[Shoulders slump and he looks at menu sadly.]

But I'm so hungry….

[Stands up and returns menu and napkin to table.]

[EXIT BOY TWO. ENTER WAITER. He/She is confused that his/her customers have gone missing. Shrugs shoulders, shakes head, and fixes table again.]

[ENTER BOY THREE and GIRL THREE. WAITER seats BOY THREE and GIRL THREE, hands them the menus, and pretends to fill their glasses with water. BOY THREE and GIRL THREE settle in and put napkins on their laps. EXIT WAITER.]

GIRL THREE

Oh, my! This is such a fancy restaurant! I've never been to a place like this!

BOY THREE

Me, neither!

[Examines menu. Swallows hard.]

Wow. Good thing I brought my piggy bank!

[Puts piggy bank on the table.]

GIRL THREE

[Stares at the piggy bank for a moment, but then returns her focus to the menu.]

OK, well, hmm…. I wonder what X-Cargo is? Sounds like a military term.

BOY THREE
I have no idea. Maybe should order some.

GIRL THREE
It's twenty dollars.

BOY THREE
[Looks apologetically at piggy bank and pets it.]
Sorry, girl.
[Shifts uncomfortably.]
Sorry!
[Takes off one shoe and sock and puts his foot up on the table. Pulls out his toenail clippers.]
I've got a nasty hangnail that keeps getting stuck in these socks! It's about to drive me crazy!
[Starts digging into his foot with toenail clippers.]

GIRL THREE
Wow. That is a nasty one, alright!

BOY THREE
[Finishes and puts his leg down.]
There! I think I got it.
[Looks around.]
But… I'm not sure where the nail went. It flew off somewhere. …Oh! There it is! It landed right in your glass!
[Hands her his glass.]
Here. You can have mine.

[GIRL THREE takes a sip of his water. BOY THREE takes the glass back from her when she's done and then takes a long drink himself.]

BOY THREE

Oh, dear.... Here it comes!
[Opens mouth.]

SOUND: DIGUSTING BURP

I'm sorry! That was a terrible burp.

GIRL THREE

You're dang right it was! You call *that* a burp? This is a burp!
[Opens mouth wide.]

SOUND: REALLY LONG DISGUSTING BURP

Now, *that's* a burp!

BOY THREE

Wow!
[Reaches for her hand and takes it.]
You are the sweetest and coolest girl I've ever met! I just know you're the girl for me!

GIRL THREE

Aw! That's so sweet! Say, this isn't really my style of place. Do you wanna get out of here? I know this great burrito place downtown.

BOY THREE

I sure do!
[Grabs his piggy bank, hugs it, and stands up.]

[EXIT BOY THREE and GIRL THREE hand in hand. ENTER WAITER. He/She is again confused that his/her customers have gone missing.]

WAITER

Why do all my customers keep leaving?

    [Takes a quick sniff under each armpit. Shrugs and walks out.]

    [EXIT WAITER.]

THE END

THE CENTURION WHO SAW TRUTH

Theme:
Easter. Dramatic Reading.

Time Duration:
5-7 minutes

Characters:

CENTURION:	The Centurion who crucified Jesus and later oversaw the guarding of the tomb. (I'm taking some creative license here for simplicity's sake and to get the whole story into one monologue. The Scriptures do not say the same man did both, but neither does it say otherwise.)

Script:

[ENTER CENTURION. He has a scroll in his hand. He reads from the scroll. (The script can be on the scroll.) He reads as if he is talking to his sister herself.]

CENTURION

To my dear sister, Ana, of Rome, from Lucius Arrius, Centurion in the Roman Army, stationed in Jerusalem. After reading this scroll, please destroy it, as it contains information that could threaten my life if leaked.

My dear sister, I write to tell you of something incredible I witnessed. This event was so amazing, I risk my own life to tell it to you, because I can remain silent no longer. I am compelled to share it, and of all people, I love you the most and want you to know the truth.

As you know I have always taken great pride in serving the Empire. In only six years I will have earned my Roman citizenship, and you and I and our families will finally be secure. In this endeavor,

I have endured many hardships and done many things I cannot share with you. I will just say that death and killing has become commonplace. Suffering—both mine and that of others—is a daily experience, and I would be lying if I told you my heart has not been hardened in the process. The cries of women and babes and of dying men no longer reach my ears. I focus on my work—work that stains my hands with blood—and I am good at it.

I confess this to you so you will understand what a great thing has occurred, for now I see clearly what I am—what I have become.

Perhaps you have heard of the one they call Jesus of Nazareth. He developed a great following among the Jewish rabble here in Jerusalem and in the countryside beyond. Indeed, even some of the wealthy and elite members of the Jewish community have followed Him, but most of the Jewish religious leaders despised him. After much scheming, the Jewish chief priests convinced Pontius Pilate to put him to death. I was ordered to crucify him.

Perhaps you will hate me for what I am about to tell you, but I did not think much of the task at the time. I have crucified many men, and my biggest concern at the time was to make sure they died in time for me to go back to the Antonia Fortress before nightfall so I could get a good meal. These executions are very tiring, for they often last days. I was happy, in fact, that the Jews insisted it be done with a certain amount of swiftness, since the Jewish Passover was upon us.

We had three to crucify that day, including Jesus. I will spare you the details, but Jesus was hung on a cross in the center, between two thieves. I carved a sign into a piece of wood that I hung above his head. It read "King of the Jews," for he had claimed to be the long awaited Jewish Messiah and, indeed, his lineage put him in direct line for the throne of David. But we did it to mock him.

As he hung there, my men and I cast lots for his robe, for it was a costly garment. The other men, in great physical and emotional distress cursed us and spat upon us. We repaid them with more suffering, but we were not surprised by their actions. For I have seen many men die at my hand and their reactions are always the same—

first they plead for their lives, then they pour contempt on us. They cry in agony, hoping their cries will elicit some kind of mercy. But they do not understand that, as members of the Roman army, we have no choice over what we do. If we do not carry out our duty— no matter what that duty is—we ourselves face death by the sword.

But Jesus was different. He behaved as if he understood us. He did not blame us for what we did to him, though his agony was as great as any other's. He never once pleaded for his life. He never once cursed us or spat upon us. Even when we demanded he carry his own cross, after having been flogged within an inch of his life, he endeavored to obey—to the last of his strength.

Still, I believed that, once Jesus was on the cross, he would recant his lies about being the Son of God. Surely, when he experienced the kind of torture we could inflict on him, he would admit he was a fraud and beg the chief priests to let him go. Instead, he forgave on of the thieves who hung on the cross next to him. He promised the man he would be with him in Paradise soon.

That is what first got my attention, but as the hour of Jesus's death drew near, something even greater happened. Though it was the middle of the afternoon on a sunny day, the whole land grew dark. Jesus cried out, "Father, into your hands I commit my spirit!" Then, he breathed his last. It was as though he actually decided when he would die. After seeing all of these things, I felt something happening inside of me. It was as if my heart had stopped beating long ago and, suddenly, it started back up again. I looked up at him and said, "Surely this was a righteous man."

Afterwards, though my experiences on the mountain had shaken me to the core, I did not know what to think of it all. But I did not have time to sort it out. My superior ordered me and the entire contingent of soldiers under my command to guard the tomb of Jesus. They claimed there were rumors that Jesus's disciples were planning on stealing the body to make it appear that Jesus had come back to life. For Jesus had claimed he would overcome the grave.

I obeyed. We took the body down from the cross and followed the small group of Jesus's family to the tomb where they placed him. We sealed the cave entrance with a rock so large it took ten of my men to move it. We rolled in along a track and then it dropped down into a divot in the ground in front of the tomb entrance. Then we roped off the stone and placed Caesar's seal on it, so that any who dared break the seal risked death. Surely that should have been enough, but my men and I stayed there to guard the tomb with our lives, not daring to sleep.

On the morning of the third day, as we paced before the tomb entrance, having seen no one approach, a violent earthquake shook the mountain. It knocked me off my feet. I looked and saw a bright light descending from Heaven. The light took the form of a man—mighty and tall. He went to the tomb and, with no effort at all, rolled the stone away. Then he sat on the stone and looked at us. I tried to move, but my fear was so great that I could not. My body would not respond and I found I could say nothing.

With my own eyes I saw the man I had crucified—Jesus of Nazareth—walk out of his grave, alive and well. He looked at me as he passed, and I saw that his hands still bore the holes I had placed there with the nails that held him to the cross. I feared he would strike me dead, but the look he gave me was one of peace. In that moment, dear sister, I knew He was indeed who He claimed to be. He is the King of the Jews, their Messiah, and the very Son of God!

Dearest Ana, all this happened only yesterday. The man we put to death lives! It is incredible to admit, but I was afraid we would be put to death for failing to keep a dead man in his grave! When my superior and the Jewish chief priests heard what had happened, they promised to spare our lives, for they believed us. Indeed, there is no way an ordinary man or even a group of men could have orchestrated such an event! But they ordered us to keep silent about what we have seen and heard.

That is why you must destroy this scroll. But I had to tell someone, and I now have one desire that is greater than all others—to find out if Jesus, who overcame death and who offers salvation to those who believe, might be willing to save me, too! I know I am the greatest of sinners, for my hands have committed horrible deeds—even against the Christ himself! But the look he gave me taught me to hope. And I cannot rest until I know if His victory over death can also be mine!

[CENTURION folds scroll, tucks it in his robe and EXITS.]

THE END

Christmas Madness

Theme:
Christmas. Song is sung to the tune of "Hark the Herald Angels Sing."

Time Duration:
3-5 minutes

Characters:

WIFE: Carries a feather duster.

HUSBAND: Caries a checkbook and a pen.

TEEN: Carries a pad of paper and a pencil.

CHILD:

Script:

[Scene opens with all CHARACTERS on stage.]

Wife:
Christmas came too soon this season,
And my patience is long gone.
I've been nagging for no reason,
And I've barked more than the dog.
Hurry up and finish eating!
It's about time you had a beating!
Why is all this mess in here?
I'll give you all a reason to fear!
Why can't I relax a bit?
Perhaps I'm too busy throwing a fit!

[At the end of the song, WIFE starts dusting things while the others sing.]

Husband:
What I wouldn't give this year,
For a little bit of cheer!

But then I found this ragged checkbook.
And I was dumb enough to look!
How could you spend that much this season?
We're all going to debtor's prison!
Two hundred fifty dollars at Ross!
How much could clothes possibly cost?
I'll have to get a second job,
…Or find a bank somewhere to rob!
> [At the end of his song he keeps looking through the checkbook, rubbing his temples and looking up like he's doing calculations in his head.]

Teen:
What might I find 'neathe that tree?
Maybe a Nintendo Wii!
Or an Ipod or a cell phone,
Or a laptop of my own!
My parents are acting kind-of funny—
But what's to fear when trees grow money?
Oh! I thought of something else!
An HD TV for that shelf.
> [Scribbles on notepad.]

This year is going to be a hit!
…As long as I get everything I list.

> [Keeps thinking of things and scribbling in notepad.]

> [As CHILD begins to sing, the others notice, guiltily stop what they're doing and slowly join in until the whole family is singing loudly and joyfully by the end of the song.]

Child:
Hark! The herald angels sing,
"Glory to the newborn King:
Peace on earth, and mercy mild;
God and sinners reconciled."
Joyful all ye nations rise,
Join the triumph of the skies;
With angelic hosts proclaim,
"Christ is born in Bethlehem!"

Hark! The herald angels sing,
"Glory to the newborn King."

[EXIT ALL.]

THE END

ƒathers Throughout History

Usage/Purpose:
To commemorate Father's Day.

Setting:
Scene opens with stage divided into four distinct sections. STAGE LEFT: Caveman dwelling. A cave wall with petroglyphs (one of a mastodon, one of a hunter, and a big smudge). One part of it painted to look like there is a hole in it. A small fake fire. A dinosaur stuffed animal attached to a stick is hidden behind cave wall. STAGE CENTER LEFT: Biblical scene. Big box painted to look like an altar. Tent-like lean-to behind that is sagging on one side. A big stick. A sheep stuffed animal or fake fish attached to a stick is hidden behind altar. STAGE CENTER RIGHT: Western scene. A fake fire pit in front of a broken coral fence behind him. A fake snake attached to a stick and an extra fence post hidden behind them. STAGE RIGHT: Modern scene. A BBQ and a couple of lawn chairs and a cooler. Plastic hotdogs in the cooler. Hammer hidden behind cooler.

Props/Preparations:
Big club   (Clubs could be made out of rolled up and spray-painted butcher paper.)
Little club
Cave wall made of cardboard with petroglyphs
Piece of cardboard painted on one side to look like a rock matching the cave wall. A big piece of masking tape is on the other side so that it will stick to the wall.
Dinosaur stuffed animal attached to a stick.
Two fake fires
Big box painted to look like an altar.
Sheep or fish stuffed animal attached to a stick.
Big fake knife

Scroll

A big stick

Lean-to that sags on one side

Fake Shotgun (made of cardboard or an empty bb-gun)

Fake snake on a stick

Broken coral post with spare post (made of cardboard)

BBQ

2 Lawn chairs

A cooler

Plastic hotdogs

Bottle of lighter fluid (empty or sealed well)

Hammer

Car keys

Lights:

Consider using a big spot light that moves to direct the audience's attention to the appropriate scene. However, this is not necessary.

Time Duration:

10-15 minutes

Characters:

ANNOUNCER: Dressed nicely in modern clothing.

CAVEMAN DAD: Dressed as a caveman. Carries a big club.

CAVEMAN
DAUGHTER: Dressed as a little cave-kid. Carries a little club.

CAVEMAN TEEN BOY: Dressed as a caveman.

BIBLICAL DAD: Dressed in biblical garb. Has a big, fake knife and a scroll tucked in the back of his belt.

BIBLICAL DAUGHTER: Dressed in biblical garb.

BIBLICAL TEEN BOY: Dressed in biblical garb.

WESTERN DAD: Dressed in western garb.

WESTERN DAUGHTER: Dressed in western garb.

WESTERN TEEN BOY: Dressed in western garb.

MODERN DAD: Dressed in modern clothing.

MODERN DAUGHTER: Dressed in modern clothing.

MODERN TEEN BOY: Dressed in modern clothing. Could make him look like a punk.

Script:

[Scene opens with all DADS and DAUGHTERS in their particular scenes.

ANNOUNCER

Welcome and thanks for joining us today on this very rare Father's Day! Why is it rare, you ask? Because on this particular Father's Day we have been given a wonderful gift—the Window to History 2000! Today this amazing device will show us the incredible impact fathers have had on their children throughout history. Let's first take a look at how fathers have provided for their families.

[Gestures to caveman scene.]

Ah! There is the faithful caveman sitting with his daughter at a warm fire he built.

CAVEMAN DAD

Mmmm…. Me hungry. Ah! I invent bar-b-q!

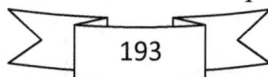

193

[Slams club behind him like he's killing something and picks up dinosaur on a stick. Roasts dino over the fire.]
Oooooo! This be good!

CAVEMAN DAUGHTER
Ew! No like dino!

CAVEMAN DAD
Shut mouth! You eat!

CAVEMAN DAUGHTER
Aw!

ANNOUNCER
And there, my friends, is a man from biblical times!

BIBLICAL DAD
Hmm… my stomach maketh unusual noises. I wonder what the Lord provideth for our supper?
[Looks around and finds sheep/fish on a stick. Starts to roast it on the altar.]
Ooooo! This will be good!

BIBLICAL DAUGHTER
Ew! I care not for sheep/fish!

BIBLICAL DAD
Be still, daughter! You will eat and be thankful!

BIBLICAL DAUGHTER
Aw!

ANNOUNCER
And there we have a man who appears to be from the American old west with his daughter at his side!

WESTERN DAD

Well, I'm so hungry I could eat my own leg! Wonder what's fer dinner?

[Looks around and finds a snake on a stick. Starts to roast it on the fire.]

Ooooo! This is gonna be good!

WESTERN DAUGHTER

Ew! I hate snake!

WESTERN DAD

Now, you shut yer mouth! Yer gonna eat it if I says so, an' I says so!

WESTERN DAUGHTER

Aw!

ANNOUNCER

Yikes! Well, let's see what our modern dad is up to.

MODERN DAD

Man, I'm hungry! I think my stomach is digesting me from the inside out!

[Rummages around in the cooler and pulls out hotdogs. Drops them on the grill.]

Man, oh, man! These are going to be good!

MODERN DAUGHTER

Ew! You know I hate hotdogs! Yuck!

MODERN DAD

Hey, no complaints! You're going to eat these hotdogs or nothing at all!

MODERN DAUGHTER

Aw!

ANNOUNCER

Ah, what touching pictures of house and home from throughout the centuries. We've seen how well fathers have been providing for their families, but now let's see how they maintain their homes.

CAVEMAN DAUGHTER

[Points to hole in cave wall.]

Ug. Wall broken.

CAVEMAN DAD

Me fix.

[Picks up rock and sticks it to the hole.]

BIBLICAL DAUGHTER

[Points to tent where it is sagging.]

Abba, our tent is broken.

BIBLICAL DAD

I will repair it.

[Picks up big stick and props up sagging spot.]

WESTERN DAUGHTER

[Points to broken fence.]

Pa, yer fence is broke!

WESTERN DAD

Let me at'er.

[Picks up fence post and sticks it into place.]

MODERN DAUGHTER

[Points to back of grill.]

Dad, the grill's broken.

MODERN DAD

Not for long!

[Picks up hammer and gives the back of the grill a whack.]

ANNOUNCER
Wow! Where would we be without dads? But I wonder how they deal with other kinds of problems—like math problems! I wonder how our fathers help their kids with their homework?

CAVEMAN
[Points to petroglyph of an animal.]
This one.

CAVEMAN DAUGHTER
Mastodon.

CAVEMAN
Good.
[Points to petroglyph of a person.]
This one?

CAVEMAN DAUGHTER
Hmmm… Hunter?

CAVEMAN
Good.
[Points to smudge.]
This one.

CAVEMAN DAUGHTER
Last night's dinner.

CAVEMAN
[Looks back at smudge. Licks it.]
Ummm! *Very* good!

BIBLICAL DAD

Now, daughter, we shall work on your memorization of the Torah!
[Pulls scroll from his belt and opens it.]
Repeat after me, "In the beginning…"

BIBLICAL DAUGHTER

[Moans.]
In the beginning.

WESTERN DAD

[Teaching daughter how to aim his shotgun.]
Now, jus' hold it right there 'gainst yer shoulder like so.

WESTERN DAUGHTER

But how do I know what to shoot?

WESTERN DAD

Well, now, you can shoot jus' about ever-thing, ceptin' yer uncle Billy.
[Laughs.]
Jus' remember this rule. If'n it's got ears bigger'n mine, we kin shoot it an' eat it. If'n it's got teeth bigger'n mine, we kin shoot it an' skin it.

MODERN DAUGHTER

Dad, my teacher said you're supposed to help me write a poem.

MODERN DAD

Roses are red, violets are blue…

MODERN DAUGHTER

[Exasperated.]
Dad!

MODERN DAD

I've already done homework, and graduated, too.

ANNOUNCER
What a special scene.

LIGHTING: STAGE LIGHTS FLICKER, BUT REMAIN ON

But, oh, dear! Looks like our Window to History 2000 is beginning to glitch out. We only have time for one last glimpse at these fathers we've come to know and love. Hmmm.... I wonder how they are as protectors?

[ENTER CAVEMAN TEEN STAGE LEFT. Approaches CAVEMAN DAD.]

CAVEMAN TEEN
Ug, ug. I here. Ask daughter on dino-ride.

CAVEMAN DAD
[Stands up, takes club, and bops CAVEMAN TEEN on the head.]

[CAVEMAN TEEN drops to ground, knocked out.]

CAVEMAN DAUGHTER
[Exasperated.]
Dad!

[ENTER BIBLICAL TEEN STAGE LEFT. Approaches BIBLICAL DAD.]

BIBLICAL TEEN
Hello, Rabbi. I have come seeking your permission to wed your daughter.

BIBLICAL DAD
Oh, what an honor for our family. ...Of course, there is one very small thing we have to take care of first.

[Pulls out big, fake knife.]
Your circumcision!

[BIBLICAL TEEN yells in fright and runs off. EXIT STAGE LEFT.]

BIBLICAL DAUGHTER
[Exasperated.]
Abba!

[ENTER WESTERN TEEN STAGE RIGHT. Approaches WESTERN DAD.]

WESTERN TEEN
Howdy, Sir! I've a'come to court yer daughter!

WESTERN DAD
[Grabs shotgun.]
I believe this'n's got teeth bigger'n mine! Let's skin it!

[WESTERN TEEN yells in fright and runs off. EXIT STAGE RIGHT.]

WESTERN DAUGHTER
[Exasperated.]
Pa!

MODERN TEEN
Hello, Sir! I've come to take your daughter out on a date!

MODERN DAD
[Turns to MODERN DAUGHTER.]
Sweetheart, go grab my pistol and the shovel. We'll put him with the others.

[MODERN TEEN yells in fright and runs off. EXIT STAGE RIGHT.]

MODERN DAUGHTER

[Exasperated.]

Dad!

ANNOUNCER

Oh, yes, folks, looks like these fathers are doing just fine!

LIGHTING: STAGE LIGHTS FLICKER AND GO OUT

And it seems our Window to History 2000 has just run out of power for today! But thanks for joining us for this exciting peak into the history of how our dads have been helping us out all along! Thank you all, and be sure to hug your dads today!

[EXIT ALL.]

THE END

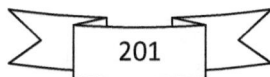

201

Mom Takes a Vacation

Usage/Purpose:
To commemorate Mother's Day.

Setting:
A living room setting with an area off to one side to resemble a kitchen. Decorate with clothes, throw pillows, and toys strewn about.

Props/Preparations:
Items to look like a mess (clothes, throw pillows, toys, etc.)
Book
Chairs (set up to look like a living room)
Small table or tray table set up with cooking supplies (pot, mixing spoon, etc.)
Smoke machine, bubble machine, OR small piece of dry ice inside a closed container. Hide this item in or behind the pot.
Cell phone

Time Duration:
8-10 minutes

Characters:
NARRATOR
MOM
DAD   Has a cell phone in pocket.
DIANA   Teen girl aged 15-18.
BRANDON   Boy aged 10-13.

Script:

[ENTER ALL. Mom is sitting reading a book in one of the chairs. DAD, DIANA, and BRANDON are standing there looking sheepish. NARRATOR stands off to the side.]

NARRATOR

It finally happened! Mom came home from work one day, found the house in a mess, and realized she was expected to clean everything up while making dinner and paying bills all at the same time. Well, to put it mildly, the woman lost her mind! To say her behavior wasn't

[Makes quote marks with fingers.]

"Christian" would be an understatement worth documenting in the annals of church history. Once she calmed down enough to speak in complete sentences fit to be heard by human ears she informed her family that she was going on vacation. So, she plopped herself down in that chair, blew the dust off her favorite book, and hasn't moved since.

What is going to happen? I wish I could tell you. Will Mom stay on vacation forever? Will Dad learn to cook an edible meal? Will the kids clean up before their family is chosen for the next episode of Hoarders: Buried Alive? I don't know. But let's peek in on them and see how things are going.

BRANDON

[Puts hands on his stomach and looks unhappy.]

There is a strange painful sensation in my middle. What is it?

DIANA

It's called hunger. We need to get something to eat!

[Turns to MOM.]

Mom, can you--?

DAD

[Interrupting and grabbing her arm to stop her.]

No, no, no! Do you want to enter World War III? Not a word to your mother! We'll figure this out. Come on. I believe food comes from this part of the house.

[Heads toward table set up to look like a kitchen.]

DIANA

I remember Mom often stirring stuff with this stick-like item.

[Holds up mixing spoon.]

BRANDON

Yeah! And then she makes it hot with this thing.

[Picks up a pot.]

DAD

Here, I will work with the heating device while you two clean up the house.

[Starts messing with things in the kitchen.]

[DIANA and BRANDON return to the living room area.]

DIANA

Hmm…. I'm trying to remember what Mom usually does with all these clothes.

BRANDON

She just throws them away.

DIANA

Yeah. I think you're right.

[BRANDON and DIANA start gathering up the clothes.]

DIANA

Wait a second…. If she throws them away, how do they end up back in our closets and drawers?

BRANDON

Maybe she buys new ones.

DIANA

She buys new clothes that are exactly like these? That can't be right.

BRANDON

Well, they can't be the same ones!
[Takes a whiff of one of the items of clothing and coughs.]
Because these really stink!

DIANA

[Holds up an item of clothing and examines it detective-style.]
Hmm…. There must be a way to get the stink out.

BRANDON

Do you think they are washable?

DIANA

Brandon, you're a genius! I remember now! Mom has something called a washing machine! I bet that's how she does it!

BRANDON

[Skeptical.]
Oh, yeah? Where is this so-called, mystery device you call a washing machine?

DIANA

It's in the basement! Come'on! I'll show you!

[DIANA and BRANDON gather up all the clothes and take them to the back of the stage where they put them in a pile. They pretend to talk quietly for a few moments before returning. Do not return until *after* the smoke starts rising.]

DAD

Alright! I think I've got it now! The meat and the green items from the cold place are now in the pot. The heating device is working! All I have to do is….

[Smoke (or bubbles) starts rising from the pot.]

Oh, no! What did I do?

[DIANA and BRANDON return.]

BRANDON

Dad! What happened?

DAD

I have no idea.

[Waves smoke away, coughs, and they all walk out of the kitchen into living room area.]

Don't worry! I'll figure it out later. But maybe we should call for pizza this time.

[Takes out phone and starts dialing. Pretends to talk in background while DIANA and BRANDON talk.]

DIANA

We should pick up the rest of this mess.

BRANDON

Wait. You mean these things don't just go here?

DIANA

No. Mom always seems to find another place for them.

BRANDON

No wonder I always have to pull everything out before I get to play with my stuff! I just thought she was trying to hide it from me!

DAD

[Puts phone back in pocket.]

OK, the pizza is on its way. I made sure to get your mom's favorite kind.

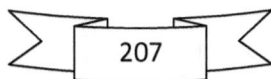

DIANA

That was a good idea, Dad. …You know, Mom always works so hard around here. Maybe it's time we started helping out a little bit.

BRANDON

But we're so bad at it!

[MOM gets up, puts down her book and comes over to them. She puts an arm around her kids and smiles.]

MOM

I don't mind if you're bad at it. I just want to see you really trying. Keeping the home running smoothly is a family job, not just a one-person job. It doesn't really even matter who does what—as long as we all work together and help each other.
[Squeezes her kids and takes DAD's hand. Smiles at them.]
And I'm sorry I blew up at you guys. That was not fair of me. Next time I'll try to respond calmly, not react in anger.

DAD

That's okay, dear. We love you and from now on we'll try to be better at showing you how much we appreciate you.

BRANDON

Yeah but next time can we go on vacation together?

[ALL laugh.]

MOM

Sure, but maybe we should keep the house from burning down first, shall we?

[ALL go to kitchen and get the smoke/bubbles turned off. EXIT ALL.]

THE END

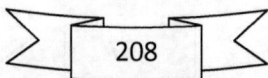

THE NEW YEAR'S RESOLUTION

Usage/Purpose:
Use to commemorate the coming new year and also to emphasize a Christ-centered attitude regarding new year's resolutions.

Props:
Huge bowl of chips/popcorn/cheeseballs

Time Duration:
2-3 minutes

Characters:
(Feel free to change names to fit actors/actresses. Gender doesn't matter.)

PEYTON: A teen boy.

KARSEN: A little boy of about 8 or 10.

Script:

[Scene opens with KARSEN sitting on the floor CENTER STAGE with huge bowl of snacks on his lap, happily munching away. ENTER PEYTON.]

PEYTON
Whoa, whoa, whoa! Where did you get that?
[Indicates bowl.]

KARSEN
Just stay back, Peyton! This is mine!
[Wraps an arm around bowl defensively but keeps eating.]

PEYTON

Karsen, you better put that back, or you're going to catch it when Mom gets home.

KARSEN

Nuh, uh!

PEYTON

There's no way she's going to let you eat that whole bowl of junk food! Especially
[Checks watch or clock or phone.]
an hour before dinner time.

KARSEN

She will, too. Because I'm just doing what the pastor said.

PEYTON

[Confused and skeptical.]
What? The pastor told you to eat a giant bowl of [fill in name of snack] in one sitting?

KARSEN

No, but he said that, when we pick a New Year's resolution, we should get ready to follow through with it. I picked no more [fill in name of snack.] So, I'm eating all I can now since I won't get any later.

PEYTON

[Laughing.]
Karsen, you can't cure a habit by over-indulging in it. I think the pastor wanted you to prepare by praying and asking God to give you the strength to stick to your commitments.

KARSEN

[Chewing more slowly.]

Really? I just have to pray?

PEYTON

Yeah, that and learn to rely on God. But I think he also said something about not picking a resolution just to pick one. And that, if we do choose one, to make sure it's one God is leading us to choose—something that has a purpose in our lives or in God's kingdom.

KARSEN

You mean, I don't have to eat all of this?

PEYTON

Definitely not.

KARSEN

[Looking sick. Moves bowl off of lap.]
Oh, good!
[Lies down on his back.]
Cause I don't feel so well.

PEYTON

[Laughing.]
Come on.
[Helps KARSEN to his feet, and begins leading him off stage.]
Let's go see if we have any Pepto Bismol.

[EXIT ALL.]

THE END

The Peace Giver

Theme:
Christmas

Setting & Props:
Several booths are set up left to right on stage. Each is manned and has a hidden label that is flipped over as the couple comes by. They are as so: Booth 1, Save the Squirrels; Booth 2, DVD Rewinders Sold Here; Booth 3, Narcolepsy Association (the person manning this booth is asleep but wakes up occasionally); Booth 4, Support the Demo-Publican Party (with a picture of a half-donkey, half-elephant); at the end of this line JESUS is standing off to the side dressed in biblical garb.

Time Duration:
5 minutes

Characters:
HUSBAND
WIFE
BOOTHKEEPER 1 (BK1)
BOOTHKEEPER 2 (BK2)
BOOTHKEEPER 3 (BK3)
BOOTHKEEPER 4 (BK4)
JESUS
READER

Script:

[ENTER HUSBAND AND WIFE stage left. They approach the first booth.]

BK1
Ah! Welcome! You look like a couple of people who care about the state of your environment!

WIFE

Why, yes, we do very much.

BK1

Wonderful! So, if you knew that small, helpless, adorable animals were being chased, hunted down, tortured, and then mercilessly killed—all for sport—wouldn't you want to do something to stop it?

HUSBAND

I suppose so.

BK1

[Gravely.]
Well, I'm sorry to tell you that it's true, my friends!
[Flips over sign.]
Won't you consider donating to the Save the Squirrels Foundation? Help stop cats everywhere from toying with these graceful creatures!

WIFE

Squirrels?

BK1

Yes! Isn't it terrible? Won't you help?

HUSBAND

But how will money make cats stop chasing squirrels?

BK1

Well, the money will fund the research to come up with a viable solution, raise awareness, and solicit further donations. Perhaps they'll come up with a cat-repellent spray, behavior altering medications for the cats, or they could even clone cats that would rather play with pigeons. The possibilities are endless, really. We take cash, VISA, MasterCard, and your personal check.
[Pushes the donation box toward them.]

WIFE

Uh, sorry. I don't think we'll be donating this year.
[Begins to move on.]

BK1

But the violence continues even to this very day!

HUSBAND

Sorry.

[HUSBAND AND WIFE move on to the next booth. As they approach BK2 flips over sign and starts calling.]

BK2

Get your DVD rewinders here! Step right up! They're going fast folks! This is the only place in town where you can get your very own DVD rewinder!

WIFE

A DVD rewinder?

BK2

Yes, Ma'am, and only for three easy payments of $19.95! You won't find a deal like this anywhere!

HUSBAND

Uh… let's hope not. Come on, honey, let's keep going.

BK2

[Calling after them.]
Come on, folks! …OK! For you, only 2 easy payments of $19.95! …Only 1?

[They move on to the next booth, and as they approach BK3 flips over sign.]

BK3

Looking for a worthy cause to support this season? Won't you consider helping fight narcolepsy?

WIFE

Well, I've heard that it can be a terrible disease.

BK3

It is, Ma'am, it certainly is. Won't you consider giving a 20, 40 or 1,650 dollars to help find a cure?

HUSBAND

Well, I don't know, we're a little stretched this year and—

BK3

Think of the suffering people, Sir!

WIFE

Well, it *does* seem like a worthy cause.

HUSBAND

[Reluctantly pulls out the checkbook.]

BK3

Oh, thank you! You're very generous! Your gift will go a long way to—

[Suddenly, he stops talking and drops down onto the table, fast asleep.]

WIFE

Sir? Sir?

HUSBAND

Shhhh! Let's not wake him.

[Returns checkbook to pocket.]

Hurry! Let's get out of here before he wakes up!

[They hurry on to the next booth. BK4 flips over sign as they approach.]

BK4

Sir! Wouldn't you agree that our nation is in serious trouble?

HUSBAND

Yes, I guess so.

BK4

Ma'am, do you agree that we need better guidance, fewer taxes, and a leader who will put the future of our children first?

WIFE

Sure.

BK4

Then, won't you consider supporting the Demo-Publican party in the upcoming election? With your votes and your cold, hard cash, we might be able to make something of this run-down, morally corrupt society we live in! Won't you join us?

HUSBAND

[Distracted by the sign.]
What kind of animal is that?

BK4

[Proudly.]
Oh! That's a Donk-phant... or an Elefonky. We're not sure what to call it yet, but don't worry. Half of each dollar you give will go to cloning one of these babies and *then* we'll figure out what to call it, for sure. Do we have your support?

WIFE

Uh... I don't think so.

HUSBAND

No. Not this year... or ever.

[They move on, to the great disappointment of BK4. They approach JESUS.]

HUSBAND

[Skeptically.]
And who are you?

JESUS

I'm Jesus.

WIFE

Oh, Jesus! It's so good to see you again!

HUSBAND

[Embarrassed.]

Oh! I'm sorry I didn't recognize you at first! I guess it's been a while since we talked. But, you know, it gets awfully busy this time of year.

WIFE

Yes… there's all the cooking and baking to be done.

HUSBAND

And shopping for Christmas presents.

WIFE

And sending out Christmas cards.

HUSBAND

And putting up Christmas lights.

WIFE

And the tree and all the decorations.

HUSBAND

[Gesturing to booths.]

And then every time we turn around, someone's trying to get something out of us.

WIFE

We're stretched really thin. We get so busy…

HUSBAND

And then we just get tired.

JESUS

Yes, I understand. But, have you, perhaps, forgotten why you keep doing all that you're doing? Have you stopped to think that perhaps you're tired because you've forgotten where your strength comes from? Have you forgotten that I am the child you see represented in the nativity scene? And that I grew up, I died for your sins, and I dwell inside you to give you the peace and the joy you now seem so desperate to find or buy?

WIFE

Oh, dear! I guess we kind-of lost sight of You in all the activity surrounding Your birthday.

HUSBAND

And we let those activities rob us of the time we spend with You— letting You fill us with the peace and the joy and the rest that only You can give. Thank you for reminding us.

WIFE

Thank you for loving us, Jesus.

HUSBAND

And most of all, thank you for coming to bring light into our darkness.

[They freeze in place as the READER enters.]

READER

"I have told you these things, so that in me you may have peace. In this world you will have trouble. But take heart! I have overcome the world." John 16:33

[EXIT ALL.]

THE END

THANKSGIVING
Isn't For Sissies!

Themes:
Thanksgiving, Peacemaking, Forgiveness

Setting & Props:
Giant Candy Bar
Gift basket made to look like it is filled with various goodies.

Time Duration:
5 minutes

Characters:

ALICE	An adult woman.
CELESTE	An adult woman.
JOEY	A boy ten-12 years old.

Script:

[ENTER ALICE and CELESTE.]

ALICE
Celeste, I'm so glad you came over to visit! I've just had such a good time talking with you today.

CELESTE
Me, too!

[ENTER JOEY. JOEY is carrying a giant candy bar but has a very sour look on his face.]

ALICE
Excuse me for a moment, Celeste. Joey, what is the matter? Why are you looking so upset? And where did you get that enormous candy bar?

JOEY

Sister gave it to me. But I'm not going to eat it!

ALICE

Well, why not? It's your favorite kind.

JOEY

Because she got mad at me yesterday for being in her room. She was mean and yelled at me, and I'm not going to forgive her!

ALICE

Well, Joey, it looks like your sister is doing her best to make it up to you. I think you should just swallow your pride and hurt feelings, go in there, and thank her for the candy bar. As brother and sister, you two should always be willing to make up. …And then you can enjoy your candy bar.

JOEY

Hmm…. OK. You're right, Mom. And you know what? I'm going to share this candy bar with her, too!

ALICE

That's my boy!

[EXIT JOEY.]

CELESTE

What great kids you have, Alice! I'm so impressed!

ALICE

Thank you!

CELESTE

But that reminds me.
[She extends the gift basket toward ALICE.]
Margo from church asked me to drop this off to you.

ALICE

Margo?

[Takes a suspicious look at the contents, but refuses to take the basket. Holds up hand.]
Oh, no! I'm not accepting that!

CELESTE
Why not?

ALICE
Margo was the one who refused to let me host the Peacemakers Luncheon last year, and now she's just trying to manipulate me by giving me that basket! Well, I'm not falling for it!

CELESTE
Hmmm…. Sounds like you got your feelings hurt.

ALICE
Yes. And I had bought a bunch of supplies and then didn't get to use them. It was such a waste! I just felt so unappreciated and like she was trying to force me out of that ministry!

CELESTE
Not unlike your daughter forced your son out of her room yesterday, huh?

ALICE
Oh, dear! You're right, Celeste! What am I doing? I just told my son it was his responsibility to be willing to make peace with his sister. And here I am refusing to forgive one of my sisters in Christ! What kind of mother am I?

CELESTE
You're a great mother, Alice, and you have great kids. It's just harder to see our own mistakes sometimes.

ALICE
Wow! Here, let me have that basket.

[CELESTE hands basket to ALICE. ALICE looks through it.]

She even included my favorite mints and the new CD album of my favorite band!

CELESTE
Looks like she's really trying to repair the rift between you.

ALICE
And who am I to stand in the way? I need to take my own advice and swallow my pride. I'm going to call her this afternoon. Thanks, Celeste, for helping me see myself clearly. I wish I was a better person.

CELESTE
You know what, Alice? We all have our blind spots. Me, too! You do what you know until you know better. When you know better, you can do better.

[ALICE and CELESTE hug one another.]

Thanks for having me over! I'll see you next Sunday!

ALICE
Bye!

[EXIT CELESTE. ALICE again looks through the basket and smiles. EXIT ALICE.]

THE END

ABOUT THE AUTHOR

S. E. Thomas, M.A.
is a multi-published, award-winning, author, editor, &
publisher. A wife, mother, and avid story-teller, she lives
and works in Lolo, Montana. She has her master's degree in
philosophy and writes biblical historical fiction, YA
dystopia, Christian drama, and Christian apologetics.
She served as Drama Team Leader at Trinity Baptist Church
in Moscow and now volunteers at church in Missoula,
Montana and works at the local Care Net Pregnancy
Resource Center.

**Please follow her author's page on Amazon and connect
with her via Facebook and Twitter at:**

www.facebook.com/authorsethomas

@susanethomas1

More From The Dramatic Pen

@TDPPress

www.TheDramaticPen.com

Facebook.com/TheDramaticPen

The Scrolls of the Nevi'im Series:

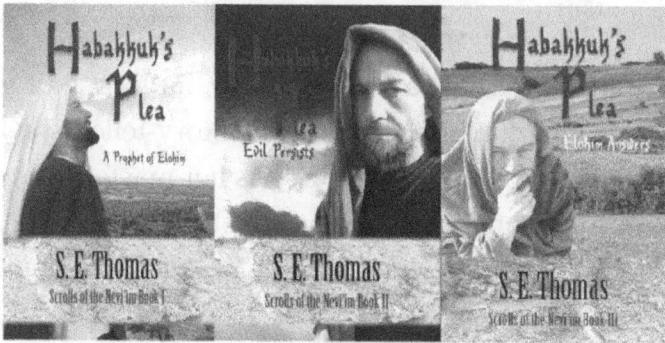

Book I: Habakkuk's Plea: A Prophet of Elohim
Book II: Habakkuk's Plea: Evil Persists
Book III: Habakkuk's Plea: Elohim Answers
By S. E. Thomas, M.A.

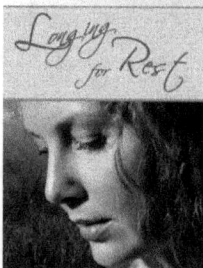

Longing for Rest
A Novella
By S. E. Thomas

One heartbroken woman battles insomnia. Another cannot escape the coma trapping her between dreams and reality. Though they have never met, through a miraculous crossing of consciousness, they find themselves together on a grassy hill surrounded by a mysterious fog. In this dream world, Amy and Gracie form an unusual friendship. But will fear, pain, and betrayal follow them and spoil this haven? Will they finally be able to rest? Can a dream change your life? Available in paperback ($7.99) or eBook ($2.99 from Kindle or Nook.)

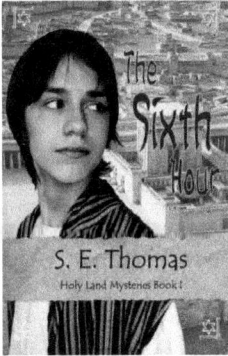

The Sixth Hour
Book I of the Holy Land Mysteries Series
By S. E. Thomas

Can Darash, a Jewish teenager, track a killer, rescue his family from ruin, and discover the truth about Yeshua? The rebel, Yeshua, drove the merchants and moneychangers from the Temple with a whip. Hours later, one of them was murdered. Now fifteen-year-old Darash must find a way to protect his family from poverty even as he struggles with the grief of losing his father. When another murder is committed, Darash finds himself searching for a dangerous killer and relying on an old, blind basket-weaver for help. Despite the odds, Darash discovers he has strength of character, a deep compassion for others, and an uncanny knack for problem-solving. But will he be able to expose the killer before the killer finds him?

The Holy Land Mysteries Series

Darash's adventures continue with…

Book II: The Brazen Altar
Book III: The Mud Flower
Book IV: The Leper's Gift
Book V: The Weeping Place

And More!

Be Inspired by Poetry from Montana Artists of All Ages

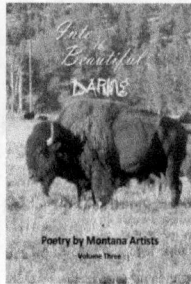

Into the Beautiful: Poetry by Montana Artists Series

"Into the Beautiful: Poetry by Montana Artists" is a series of poetry books by Montana artists of all ages. These works of art and creativity were collected through annual contests run August through October 15th. To find out more about this contest, please visit our website at www.TheDramaticPen.com.

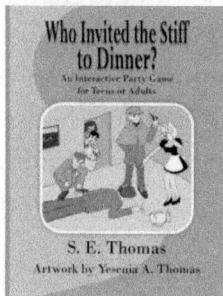

Throw a Mystery Party!

**Who Invited The Stiff to Dinner?
An Interactive Mystery Party Game
for Teens and Adults
By S. E. Thomas**

The guests arrive for a distinguished dinner party at the wealthy English estate of Richard Orwell Mortice. But why would he invite so many of his enemies into his home, along with a Scotland Yard Inspector? When the maid discovers good ol' Rick O. Mortice dead, the Inspector and his overly eager Lieutenant sidekick are out to discover the culprit! Everyone has a motive, and the accusations fly—but not before they go ahead and sit down to a luxurious meal. After all, why let one stiff ruin dinner? *(Requires 15 participants. Includes full, reproducible script, invitation templates, nametags, place settings, and a full set of host/hostess directions. Templates available online for free download.)*

Murder at Surly Gates

An Interactive Mystery Party Game for Teens and Adults
By S. E. Thomas

Murder at
Surly Gates
An Interactive Party Game
for Teens or Adults

S. E. Thomas
Artwork by Yesenia A. Thomas

Tensions are high when the cantankerous residents of Surly Gates Nursing Home have to put up with money-hungry relatives, a spoiled brat, and her incompetent mother during visitors' hours. When the nursing home manager turns up dead in his office, everyone is a suspect! Who had something to gain from his death? What happened to Badger's heart pills? Why does Lily, a former beauty queen, still try to swing her hips—even behind her walker? Buster, a resident and former security guard, and his son, Doyle, a bumbling cop, want to solve this case! *(Requires 15 participants. Includes full, reproducible script, invitation templates, nametags, place settings, and a full set of host/hostess directions. Templates available online for free download.)*

Accuracy
An Interactive Mystery Party Game
for Teens or Adults
By S. E. Thomas

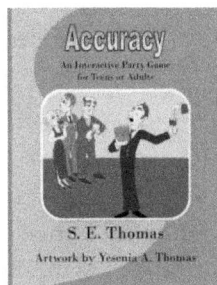

Accuracy
An Interactive Party Game
for Teens or Adults

S. E. Thomas
Artwork by Yesenia A. Thomas

A successful, but pompous, author is murdered on the night of his new book debut celebration. A note—intended to stop the murder—actually spurns the killer into action due to some rearranged punctuation. Who wrote the note? Who tampered with the note? Who carried out the false instructions? Nearly everyone has a motive! An intelligent Spanish lawyer with a very thick accent discovers the truth. *(Requires 11 participants. Includes full, reproducible script, invitation templates, nametags, place settings, and a full set of host/hostess directions. Templates available online for free download.)*

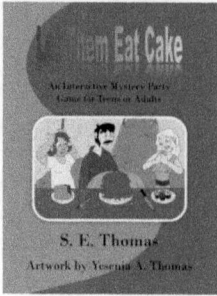

Let Them Eat Cake
An Interactive Mystery Party Game for
Teens or Adults
By S. E. Thomas

A reputable cake-baking contest is underway and the contestants are vying to win 20% of the stock in the wealthy contest sponsor's restaurant business. Then the sponsor turns up dead! He ate an entire cake ridden with arsenic-bearing apple seeds! Who gave him the cake? Who wanted him dead? Why in the world didn't he stop at the first bite? A bumbling security guard who is allergic to flour is on the case! *(Requires 14 participants.)*

A Full-Length Christmas Production for
Your Church or Christian School!

A Reason To Celebrate
A Full-Length Christmas Production
By S. E. Thomas

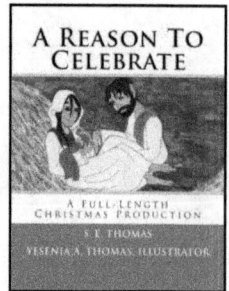

For most, Christmas is a time filled with joy. But for many, Christmas can be a difficult season. Some of us may even feel that Christmas is not a time of celebration, but of sorrow…. But let us consider a moment what Scripture tells us of the first Christmas. What really happened? For the first time, God Himself—the Creator of the Universe, the King of Kings, the Everlasting Father—stepped into our world! He stepped in—not to enjoy the wealth or the beauty or the joys—but to experience our suffering, our longings, and our sorrows. And, even from the moment of His birth, He experienced far from ideal circumstances. And yet, we remember His words, "In this world you will have trouble. But take heart! I have overcome the world."

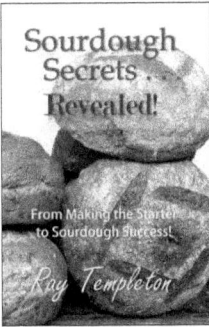

Sourdough Secrets... Revealed!
From Making the Starter to Sourdough Success!
By Ray Templeton

Step-by-step instructions that will allow you to make your own starter, make your first loaf, and even learn to make sourdough bread in your bread machine.

Is My Faith My Own?
A Resource for Christian Young People
Leaving Home for the First Time
By S. E. Thomas

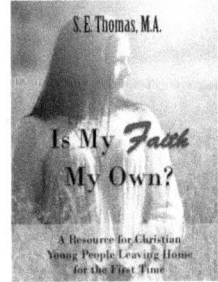

Everything was going along fine... then you got out on your own and realized it's your responsibility to get the rest of your life right. From here on out, if you're going to follow God, you're going to be doing it on your own. You can no longer coast by on your parents' faith, your pastor's understanding, or your youth leader's morals. Now it's up to you. And you have some questions: Is my faith real? Is it growing? Is it my own? (A *Finding Hope Resource Guide*.)

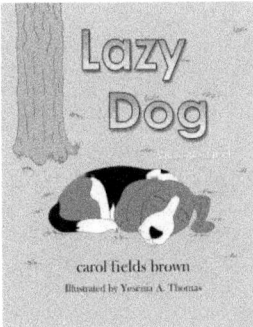

Lazy Dog
A Read-Aloud-Book
By carol fields brown

The Lazy Dog and the Fox start us on an animal adventure. This coloring book provides an opportunity for young learners to explore the intricacies of the English language, practice their handwriting, and explore a variety of animal behaviors in a fun and creative way. Full-color illustrations, matching coloring pages, and lines for handwriting practice are also included.

Please Visit Us Again!

Find books, study guides, plays, skits, mystery party games, fundraising resources, free downloadable program templates, writers' resources, and much more at:

www.TheDramaticPen.com
Write To Bless The World

www.ingramcontent.com/pod-product-compliance
Lightning Source LLC
LaVergne TN
LVHW051229080426
835513LV00016B/1482